Christians
with
Courage

by
Ruth Johnson Jay

ACCELERATED CHRISTIAN EDUCATION®
SCHOOL OF TOMORROW®
Hendersonville, Tennessee

Accelerated Christian Education
P.O. Box 299000 • Lewisville, Texas 75029-9000
P.O. Box 2707 • Hendersonville, Tennessee 37077-2707

Reprinted 2016
©2003 Accelerated Christian Education,® Inc.
with permission of Mrs. Ruth Johnson Jay

ISBN 978-1-56265-075-9
6 7 8 9 10 Printing/Year 20 19 18 17 16
Printed in the United States of America

FOREWORD

The Bible contains stories of many great men and women of God. Hebrews 11 and the Book of Acts review the lives and deeds of several Old and New Testament heroes. All were courageous and bold. Some endured great hardships. Some gave their lives for their faith. Others just consistently served their Lord and Master, spreading the Gospel and trusting His leadership.

You are about to read sketches of the lives and deeds of fourteen more modern heroes of the faith. They, too, are worthy of recognition for their contributions and furtherance of the Gospel of Jesus Christ. Like all true Christian heroes, they endured trials but demonstrated courage and faith when confronted with danger and personal sacrifice. Christian courage is not always understood by the world, but it is never overlooked by God.

TABLE OF CONTENTS

Chapter   Page

James Hudson Taylor

Long before J. Hudson Taylor was born, his mother and father dedicated him to the Lord, for they had read in Exodus 13, "Sanctify unto me all the firstborn." They knew that this meant not only the possessions in the field, but everything in their home and family. On May 21, 1832, in Yorkshire, England, a son was born, and they named him James Hudson Taylor.

From those very early days Hudson Taylor was taken to church. One of his earliest recollections was that of seeing his grandfather and grandmother seated directly behind him and his parents.

Much of Hudson Taylor's education came from home. His father taught him the Hebrew alphabet, and before he was four years old his mother taught him to read and write.

Like many other children, Hudson Taylor and his brother and sister often "played church." Their father's chair was the pulpit, and their favorite subject was the darkness of heathen lands. This is what they heard in both church and home.

"When I am a man," Hudson would say, "I plan to be a missionary and go to China."

At the Taylor home, they had a practice that pennies had to be worked for. Hudson's mother and father felt that their children needed to know and understand the value of money and realize that it could only be earned. So, little jobs around the house became their duties. One day a fair came to town. Hudson Taylor had saved a whole penny, which seemed to him like a fortune. He decided to spend it on the fair. However, when he arrived there, he found a gate at the entrance to the fairground where an admission had to be paid. He took his penny and stepped up to the man at the entrance; but the man just shook his head. The fair was two pennies.

"I don't have another penny," he said, "but I'll give you this one if you'll let me in. Wouldn't it be better for you to have one penny than none at all?" The man was unimpressed, and Hudson Taylor went home sobbing as though his heart would break. His mother put him to work so he could earn another penny, and he was soon able to attend the fair. Through this experience J. Hudson Taylor never forgot the value of money.

The Taylor children were taught that they must not ask for things at the table. One day when there was company for dinner, Hudson's plate was overlooked. For some time he sat there saying nothing. Finally when there was a pause in the conversation, he asked that the salt be passed. The guest sitting next to him looked down at his plate and said, "And what do you want the salt for?" Hudson told the dinner guest that he wanted to be ready when his mother put the food on his plate.

J. Hudson Taylor was always interested in reading. Many times he was not able to finish a book in the daylight hours and wished that he could read at night, but his mother always came to tuck him in and take the light away. One day he found an especially good story. He remembered that there were some small candle ends for use in the cellar. It would never be noticed if he took a few of these. He could light them and read in bed.

That night shortly before he was to go to bed, company arrived at the house. Hudson had already slipped the candles into his pocket when he went in to say goodnight. However, the visiting man took the boy and put him on his knee and began telling him a story. As much as Hudson loved stories, he fidgeted and squirmed most of the time. As soon as the story came to an end, he tried to jump off the man's lap. He could just imagine the candle ends melting in his pocket, for he was sitting very near the fire. Just as he was about to jump off, his mother explained that it was still early so he could stay up longer.

Again the man began to tell a story, and again Hudson Taylor squirmed and moved and finally managed to jump off the man's lap. The visitor was very disappointed and

Hudson's parents were extremely puzzled. As he went to his room, his mother followed him. There she found a weeping boy with a pocketful of melted candles. This too was an experience J. Hudson Taylor did not forget.

Since Mrs. Taylor was the children's teacher, she watched carefully as they read their history, literature, and other books. Whenever they found a word that they did not know, they had to go to the dictionary to look it up.

Punctuality was one of the lessons that Hudson Taylor learned from his mother and father. "If there are five people," his father would say, "and they are kept waiting one minute, do you not see that five minutes are lost and can never be found again?"

The spiritual life of young Taylor was encouraged and strengthened through his father. Every day during his early years, J. Hudson Taylor went to his father's room for prayer and Bible study. He was also taught to have private devotions. Before long he learned to spend some time before breakfast and again in the evening in reading God's Word and in prayer.

Because Hudson Taylor was sickly, he was unable to go to school to receive a regular education. But his classes with his mother were conducted on a systematic basis, and as a result, J. Hudson Taylor was far more advanced in his education than those who were attending school.

In the Taylor home, foreign missions was a continued subject of conversation and prayer. Hudson's father had a particular burden for China and talked and prayed about it a great deal. When Hudson was seven years old, a special jubilee was conducted, at which time thank offerings were taken and worldwide prayer offered. After this jubilee, Hudson's father remarked that a number of new workers had been sent out, but not one went to China. This, together with the reading of the book, *China*, by Peter Parley, made a definite impression on J. Hudson Taylor. Mr. and Mrs. Taylor, however, had given up hope that Hudson would be able to follow his wishes because he was always sickly.

As he grew older, his health seemed to improve, so he was able to attend school. Here, he not only missed the spiritual atmosphere of his home, but the busyness of his school schedule resulted in his putting aside the things of the Lord. He no longer found time for prayer and Bible reading as he had at home. As a result, his spiritual life began to decline. Between the years of eleven and seventeen, James Hudson Taylor lived a wavering Christian life. At the age of fifteen he was offered a job as a junior clerk in one of the banks. Here, he found things quite difficult, not only as a new worker, but because of the friends he made there. Most of them laughed at his religious and old-fashioned beliefs. It was also here that he began to feel the want and need for worldly possessions.

Again the Lord had His hand on Hudson Taylor, and because of a series of inflammations in the eyes, he had to quit his job at the bank. He went back home to work with his father; but since things were not right spiritually, he found it difficult to converse with either his mother or father. It was a little easier to talk to his sister, Emilia, who was now thirteen years old. Emilia decided she would pray for her brother three times a day. She was so determined that she wrote in a journal that she would never cease to pray for him until he was brought to the Lord Jesus Christ.

One day when his mother was away, Hudson went into his father's library to find some books. It seemed he could find nothing, so he turned over a basket of pamphlets and picked up a gospel tract. At this very same time, his mother, who was seventy or eighty miles away, got up from the dinner table and went to her room. There she locked the door, determined not to leave until she knew that her prayers for her wayward son were answered. Hour after hour she pled with God until all at once she could pray no more. She then began thanking the Lord for the conversion of her boy.

At home James Hudson Taylor decided to go ahead and read the tract. "I will just read the story. I will stop when it comes to the sermon."

But he soon found that he had not only finished the story, but he had read the sermon too. The tract told about the Lord Jesus, who willingly gave His life for the whole world.

Suddenly Hudson had a strange thought. If Jesus died for everyone in the world, then everyone should know about it. This meant that someone would have to tell them. Falling on his knees, he gave himself to the Saviour.

When his mother returned, Hudson met her to tell of his conversion. "I know," was the only thing his mother could say. Hudson Taylor thought that his sister Emilia had broken her promise and had talked to her mother about Hudson, but Mrs. Taylor assured her son that this was not so. God had spoken to her.

After Hudson Taylor gave his heart and life to the Lord, there was a definite change in his life, not only in his attitude toward those at home, but also in his attitude toward the needs of others. One day he set aside an hour for prayer when he definitely consecrated his life to God to be used for some special service. From that day on, he and his sister, Emilia, used every Sunday evening for a time of witnessing. They had been used to attending the Sunday evening service but felt they must sacrifice this in order to reach some of the people they could not reach any other time.

When Hudson Taylor was seventeen and a half years old, he knew God had called him to China. It was shortly after this that he began preparing for his work on the mission field. The first thing he did was try to improve his health. He began to exercise and spend more time in the open air. He put aside his feather bed in order to prepare for a rougher life. Tract distribution, teaching a Sunday school class, and visiting the poor and sick were on his regular list of duties.

Even though he did not have a book to teach him Chinese, he did have a copy of the writing of St. Luke in Chinese. From that he spent hours studying the Chinese language. With the help of a cousin, Hudson Taylor was able to write a Chinese dictionary with some 500 characters.

At the age of nineteen, he left home to receive more medical and surgical instruction, which he felt would be beneficial on the field. So intent was he upon going to China that he determined to work and save money toward his passage.

Finally the day came, and Hudson Taylor got on a ship going to China. Since this was a sailing ship, strong, steady winds were needed to get them where they were going. One day, while they were out in the middle of the ocean, the wind stopped blowing.

"We have done everything there is to do," said the captain to Hudson Taylor.

"No," said Taylor. "There are four Christians on this ship. We will ask God to send us a wind right away." The four men went to their cabins and began to pray. Soon a strong wind came up, and the ship began to move once more. Everyone on board was surprised—except the four men who had prayed. They knew God could send the wind.

The trip was anything but easy. In fact, it was almost disastrous. The ship had been caught in stormy weather, a cyclone, and blinding snow, but finally after five and one-half months, it reached Shanghai, China.

Instead of doing a great deal of missionary work in China as Hudson Taylor had hoped, he found himself hampered in the work. This was especially true when a war broke out between the foreign troops and the Imperial army. It was not safe for any European to be out without a gun. This distressed the young missionary because he had come to China knowing that God had sent him there to bring the message of salvation to the people. There were other discouraging things too. His eyes that had once been inflamed (while working at the bank at home) became inflamed again. The sunshine and dust caused the inflammation, and as a result, Hudson had severe headaches. In spite of this, he worked on learning the Chinese language for about five hours each day. In addition to his language study, he also continued his studies in medicine and chemistry so that he would not lose the medical touch that he felt he needed to reach the people.

Almost a year after he left home, J. Hudson Taylor was finally able to help some of the people with medical solutions, and things began to look up for him. He started a day school and had ten boys and five girls with a Christian teacher to instruct them. Even though he had not announced the opening of a dispensary, every day brought in many patients. The prayer meetings were growing too. At first, just he and his teacher attended, but before long there were as many as twenty; some coming in the morning and others in the evening. But one problem after another continued to discourage the missionary—a place to stay, food to eat, money enough to live, war in the land, and many other problems.

After some time, Hudson Taylor and another missionary rented a houseboat in which they traveled the rough waters of the Yangtze River. One day Hudson Taylor went to shore to preach to the people of a certain island. He was just about to start his sermon when he heard noises from behind the boat. Turning around, he saw hundreds of natives crowding all the way from the mainland right into the water. They looked like a swarm of bees as they crowded around him to hear the Gospel. To keep from being mobbed, he pushed back farther into the water, but this did not help. The people wanted to know what Hudson Taylor was doing, so they plunged into the water after him. He spent the rest of the afternoon telling them about the Lord Jesus.

Taylor decided that the only way he could really reach the people of China was to identify with them. He bought some Chinese clothing and began using chopsticks to eat his food. But there was still one big step that he had not taken—his blond curly hair betrayed him as a European. Because he felt it was the only way to really reach the Chinese people, he finally took the step. He called in a barber and had his hair cut, leaving only enough to make it look like the head of a Chinaman. All of this gave him an entrance into the hearts of the people, many of whom did not suspect that he was a European until he began to talk.

However, when J. Hudson Taylor received a letter from home, he learned that his family was not at all happy with what he had done. He wrote back explaining that what he did was in order to reach the Chinese for Christ, and it was proving to be very effective.

When war broke out between China and England, almost all of the people who were considered foreigners in the country found that their lives were in danger. But because he had taken on the attire and look of the Chinese, Taylor again found it easier to mingle with them. But many times his life, too, was endangered.

While in China, he met a young lady who was a teacher-missionary. She too had given her life to be used in China. Since this girl was an orphan, Hudson Taylor wrote to her uncle in Scotland asking for permission to marry her. More than two months passed before he received an answer, but when it came, the uncle had given his approval. The only thing he asked was that they wait until Marie was twenty-one.

On January 16, 1858, Marie Dyer celebrated her twenty-first birthday, and on January 20, she and Hudson Taylor were married. Now the work for the Taylors expanded. She took on children's and women's meetings and invited the nationals to come into their home. Hudson's work as an evangelist, preacher, and medical worker kept him busy day and night. More wars, famines, and problems faced them day after day and year after year, but God used Mr. and Mrs. J. Hudson Taylor to form a new mission, the China Inland Mission, and to prosper in His work. God also blessed their home with a little girl whom they named Grace.

The life of J. Hudson Taylor was a life of prayer and dependence on God. Nothing was done without first kneeling and asking that God's divine will be shown. This was true when Taylor was a young man seeking God's wisdom with regard to going to China. This was true in every evangelistic and medical journey that he took up the river reaching the interior of the country. This was done in seeking God's will in his marriage. And this needs to be done by each of us in every decision we make, large or small. For since we belong to Christ, we need to know what His perfect will is for us.

When J. Hudson Taylor knew that his work in China would soon be over, that he did not have long to live, he said to some of his friends: "Had I a thousand lives, China would claim every one."

Wilfred Grenfell

The land of Labrador can hardly be mentioned without the name of Dr. Wilfred Grenfell. It was through his efforts that the people there received medical help, started their first schools, were encouraged to learn farming, were taught to work with crafts, and, above all, learned the message of salvation in Christ Jesus.

Wilfred Grenfell was born on February 28, 1865, in Parkgate, England. His father was the head of a boarding school, which required so much of his attention that Wilfred and his brother had opportunity to go out and do many things without their father's supervision. Wilfred used his summers to investigate the countryside. He inherited the Grenfells' love for the sea, so it was natural for him to have an interest in adventure, travel, and sailing. Because of this, the two boys became acquainted with some fishermen and often went out on a fishing vessel for several days at a time. When Wilfred was fourteen years old, he was sent away to school; but by the time he was sixteen he had to leave because of lung trouble. For several months he lived with an aunt in France during the winter, and then returned to England in the summer.

When Wilfred was eighteen, his father accepted a call to do religious work in London and became chaplain of the large London Hospital. Since he was a minister, he thought his son would follow in the same footsteps. But at eighteen Wilfred showed a distinct interest in medicine.

One day while visiting the family physician, Wilfred observed a human brain which had been chemically preserved. He was deeply impressed with the thought that this organ gave direction to all the functions of the body. His search for a career had ended; he was determined now to be a doctor.

He entered as a student at the medical school maintained by the London Hospital. With high hopes for the future, he began his studies.

As a young man, Grenfell accepted Christ as his personal Saviour during a campaign conducted by Evangelist D. L. Moody. Wilfred knew that he would either have to live for Christ or forget this life of religion. After hearing the testimony of C. T. Studd, the famous cricketer, Grenfell decided to courageously make his stand for Christ.

Immediately after his conversion, he took a class of boys in a Sunday school and began to teach them. On Sunday evenings he went with an Australian doctor to hold meetings in some of the poorer sections of London. Here he saw what poverty was doing to those people. Their condition touched his heart very deeply.

While continuing his training as a surgeon at the London Hospital, Wilfred met Sir Frederick Treves. Under this famous doctor the young intern was made responsible for a number of surgical patients. In 1886 he graduated and was made a member of the College of Physicians and a similar organization for surgeons.

Not long after, new doors of opportunity opened to Grenfell. Each summer hundreds of small fishing vessels went into the North Sea for weeks at a time. This meant that several thousand men lived on the ships. They had no Christian instruction. There was not even a doctor to take care of them in times of sickness, accident, or near-death. The Royal National Mission to Deep Sea Fishermen asked the young doctor if he would serve on a hospital and mercy ship and sail with the fleet. He agreed; in fact, nothing pleased him more than this. It gave him not only an opportunity for sea travel but also a chance to serve his Master in Christian work.

Even though Wilfred Grenfell was not the first Christian missionary to work with the Inuit of Labrador, he was the first doctor to arrive there. When the first summer was over, he was convinced that a hospital was desperately needed for the onshore patients, fishermen, and Inuit alike. He also saw the great need for a hospital ship to cruise along the shores of Labrador and bring the patients to the hospital.

When Dr. Grenfell returned to London some time later, he told the people that St. John's businessmen had promised to build two hospitals in Labrador for his use. On his next trip, two medical assistants and two nurses returned with him to minister to the people he loved so well.

Grenfell established his headquarters at St. Anthony, where he erected an excellent hospital and staffed it with the best doctors he could find. From this center he sailed up and down the coasts of Newfoundland and Labrador, tirelessly caring for the sick and conducting gospel meetings.

Grenfell was concerned about the desperate lack of education in Labrador, so he founded a school at St. Anthony. This served as a model for the public schools that were later organized in almost all of the settlements. He also organized a chain of cooperative stores where the people of Labrador could buy their supplies and barter their furs and fish. He brought 300 reindeer from Lapland and transported Lapps with them as herders, so that the people of Labrador could have food and clothing.

Not only did Dr. Grenfell travel on the fishing vessels and do his medical work with fishermen, but he also spent a great deal of time traveling by dogsled. On one occasion, he received word that he was desperately needed in order to save the life of a dying boy. As he and his dog team began their journey over the frozen sea, the thin ice began to break, and he and the dogs slipped into the cold Atlantic. Finally Grenfell dragged himself and his dogs onto a small piece of floating ice. He did not have enough warm clothing with him to endure being stranded for any length of time. To keep from freezing to death, there was only one thing to do: kill three of his dogs and use their skins to keep himself warm and dry. He hesitated for some time, but finally had to do so. He fastened the hind legs together to form a flagpole on which he hung his old football jersey. He waved this constantly during the morning, and by late afternoon thought he saw a boat approaching. Finally he spotted a vessel with several men.

As a result of this trip, Grenfell spent a number of days in the hospital at St. Anthony. As soon as he recovered, he put up a bronze plaque in memory of his dogs with the inscription: "Whose lives were given for mine on the ice."

Because of the intense cold and because of disease, many people died, leaving their children orphans. When Dr. Grenfell saw this, he put up buildings to care for these children. In addition to the orphans, a number of children were taken in whose families could no longer afford to feed them. A school was conducted for them and they were soon taught to read and write. They were also taught the things of the Lord.

Until this time, Dr. Grenfell had been too busy to think about getting married. However, on one of his trips home, he met Anne MacClanahan, and on November 18, 1909, they were married in Chicago. A few months later Dr. Grenfell and his bride returned to Newfoundland. She proved to be a blessing in his work and was able to take many of the burdens from his shoulders. She had rare gifts for organization, a patience which balanced her husband's impulsiveness, and unlimited energy. God blessed their marriage by giving them three children.

One of the greatest problems in the country of Labrador was the number of shipwrecks each year. These not only meant danger and injury to the people but also often meant a great deal of food was lost on each ship. Since Grenfell felt that God had sent him not only to preach the Gospel but to heal the sick as well, he decided he had to work out something to prevent the ships from losing so much cargo through these wrecks. From money given by interested friends, a dry dock was built into which damaged ships could come to be repaired. This meant a saving of many, many vessels and also of hundreds of dollars of food each year.

Since the summers were very short in Labrador (too short to plant vegetables), Dr. Grenfell taught the people to plant seeds under glass. By July, when the ground began to thaw, they were able to put out plants that were three months old. Dr. Grenfell was so successful in this that green vegetables began to be produced in large quantities. Greenhouses were put up and food became more plentiful in the country.

Up to this time there were few hospitals in Labrador, but through the tireless efforts of the doctor, hospitals and nursing stations began to crop up in one place and another. Since complete hospitals could not be built in very many places, small nursing stations were put between the hospitals. These took care of patients who were too sick to travel all the way to the hospital. More nurses began to come to Labrador to treat the sick. Often they would go out into the country to take care of their patients, sometimes walking ten to twenty miles a day.

As the patients were recovering from their illnesses, Dr. Grenfell taught them trades. Some began to make pottery, some to weave baskets, and others to do beadwork.

While the doctor's health had been very good during the years of his ministry, when he reached the age of seventy, he suffered a heart attack. Because of this he had to retire from his work and move to his home in Vermont, though he continued to visit in Labrador from time to time. He spent his days writing about the hospital work and painting watercolors of the coast. He lectured and showed his pictures of Labrador to clubs, churches, schools, and resorts.

When Dr. Grenfell died in October 1940, his body was laid to rest beside his wife, in the land he loved so much and where he had worked for more than 40 years. As a result of his intense ministry in this frozen land, a number of missionaries are now serving the Lord and continuing the work Grenfell began.

H. A. Ironside

It was evident from the very first that God had something special planned for the life of Henry (Harry) A. Ironside. Even on the day of his birth, October 14, 1876, God performed a miracle. The doctor who attended Henry's mother thought that the baby was born dead, so quickly turned to give his special attention to the mother who was very sick. Forty minutes later a nurse discovered a slight pulse beat in the baby. Immediately the doctor worked on the child until he was pronounced "out of danger."

Two years later Henry had a little brother who was named John Williams Ironside, Jr. When John was only three weeks old, the daddy of the Ironside home died from typhoid.

Henry Ironside came from a Godly home. From his earliest days he learned the meaning of complete trust in God for his needs. The Scriptures began to take an important place in his life. His father had been known as "The Eternity Man." He was given this name because he so often stopped people and asked them where they were going to spend eternity.

A widow at the age of twenty-six, Sophia Ironside found it necessary to take in sewing in order to support her family. God blessed this work and before long she not only had enough work for herself, but had to hire other people to help her in her business.

There were days, at first, when there was no food in the house. One time she told her boys to sit down at the table and together they would ask God to bless the food. The food? There was no food. There was only water. So Mrs. Ironside gave thanks to God for the water and asked Him to provide some bread. She had hardly said, "Amen," when someone was at the door. A man, whose wife had owed Mrs. Ironside some money for sewing, brought in two bushels of potatoes to pay for the work that had been done. It took Mrs. Ironside only a few minutes to put the potatoes in the pan. God had sent food for her family! H. A. Ironside (he was usually called Harry, even though his name was Henry) saw many such miracles while Sophia Ironside's business was beginning and growing.

At the age of three, Harry began to memorize Scripture. When he was fourteen, he had completed his fourteenth reading of the Bible, though he had not yet accepted Christ as his Saviour.

Harry Ironside was born in Toronto, Canada. At the age of ten, he, his brother, his mother, and his uncle, moved to Los Angeles, California. There he was surprised to find that many people did not respect Sunday as the Lord's Day. He saw many drunk persons; he also saw gambling and many other evil practices going on. As a result of seeing these things, Ironside decided to call the boys and girls of the neighborhood together and organize a Sunday school. He sent the boys out to collect all the sacks and burlap bags they could find. For the girls he organized a sewing club. They sewed the burlap bags together and in a short time a burlap tent Sunday school began that accommodated nearly a hundred people.

Since there was no other teacher, Harry became the teacher. During the first year, sixty people attended this Sunday school. But in spite of organizing the school, teaching the lessons, and reading the Bible regularly, Harry Ironside still did not know if he had ever accepted Christ as his personal Saviour. Since he had been brought up in a Christian home, he thought he was a Christian. He felt that everyone should know the Bible, and considered himself a missionary among these people to teach it to them. He was quite proud of his religion and his familiarity with the Bible because others knew so little about it.

D. L. Moody had come to Los Angeles to conduct a campaign when Harry was twelve. One night young Ironside came late to the meeting; there was not an empty seat anywhere. He went up to the second balcony and placed himself on one of the rafters. Even that far from the preacher, he was deeply stirred by Moody's message. When

Ironside listened to D. L. Moody preach, he had only one desire: "to someday be a preacher like this and lead souls to Christ." Little did he realize at that time that he would one day become the pastor of the church that Dwight L. Moody founded.

Several things about Moody's preaching impressed Harry that night though he was still unsaved. Moody spoke for about thirty-five minutes; he quoted many Scripture passages, using illustrations that were homely and tender. He pressed on his hearers the importance of definite personal faith in the Lord Jesus Christ as Saviour.

One night in February 1890, after attending a party, Harry Ironside suddenly realized his real need for the Saviour. He remembered how a minister had once asked, "Aren't you putting the cart before the horse?" When Harry Ironside asked him what he meant, the minister explained that he was teaching from the Bible and working in a religious realm without ever having accepted Christ as his Saviour. He saw, as never before, his awful guilt before God, the blackness of his sins, and the hardness of his heart in refusing to put his trust in Christ. As soon as he could, he hurried home, for he wanted to be alone in his room. There, at the age of 14, in his own bedroom, he prayed, "Lord, save me."

From the very moment of his conversion he wanted to tell it to others. Harry Ironside's first testimony was given three days later in a street meeting. He attended a Salvation Army meeting and while listening to a Captain give his testimony, he could hardly wait until the man finished. As soon as the Captain was done, Harry stepped up and said, "Captain, may I give a testimony?"

The Captain asked him if he was saved.

"Yes," said Ironside.

"How do you know?" asked the Salvation Army officer.

"Because I have trusted the Lord Jesus as my Saviour."

"For how long?"

"Three days."

"Fire away!" said the Captain, and that is just what Harry Ironside did.

Reading from Isaiah 53:6, "All we like sheep have gone astray," Harry Ironside preached his first sermon after becoming a Christian. The very next day he led his first convert to Christ. This convert, who was a man about seventy years old, had heard young Ironside's testimony. Afterwards, he asked Harry some questions. As a result the young Christian talked to the man about his soul and led him to the Lord. The old man never forgot it. As time went on, he followed Harry wherever he preached and would say proudly, "Friends, this boy is my spiritual father."

Even though Harry Ironside had been saved for four days, he had not yet told his mother about his conversion.

One night as she was on her way to play the organ for a mission service, she asked a man if he would like to know Christ as his Saviour. The man explained that he wanted to go up and hear the "little preacher" up the street. When Mrs. Ironside found that her son was the "little preacher," she was disturbed. When she confronted her son with it that evening, he said, "I only gave my testimony."

"But," said Mrs. Ironside, "nobody has a right to do that unless he is saved."

"But I am saved, Mother," said Harry Ironside, and then he went on to tell about his conversion.

It was about this time that Mrs. Ironside remarried. William D. Watson, the stepfather of John and Harry Ironside, was very kind to the boys. He encouraged Harry to continue his schooling, not only to finish high school but also to go on to college. But Harry felt that he must get a job and also preach. Even though he did not attend a school of formal education, he continued to educate himself by reading many books. He was an avid reader, and at an early age had a fair-sized library.

An example of his mental drive and discipline during those early years is seen in the arrangement he made with a Chinese doctor. They spent two hours each week, the doctor teaching Harry Chinese and Harry teaching the doctor English.

Only a few months after his conversion, Ironside joined the Salvation Army. Before long he was given the rank of Junior Sergeant Major and put in charge of their children's work. At the age of sixteen, he was encouraged to attend their training school for a course preparatory to full officership. So he quit his job as a photographer to go to their school in San Diego, California, and he was later commissioned a Lieutenant in the Salvation Army. After spending some six years with them, he left and joined the Plymouth Brethren.

On January 5, 1898, Henry Allan Ironside and Helen Georgia Schofield were married. She was a former Salvation Army captain who had been pianist for many special meetings in which Ironside had a part. Things were quite difficult for Harry and Helen, for they had very little money. This was something that Helen was not used to. She had been brought up in a home of moderate means and was accustomed to many things that Harry was not able to provide for her. They were called upon again and again to exercise faith in God for their daily needs. The road was not easy, and there were times when the cupboard was bare.

One time when Helen's mother came to visit them, she noticed that they had beans for every meal of the day. The young bride tried to explain this by saying, "Harry is very fond of beans." In order not to offend his new mother-in-law, Harry Ironside began to ask the Lord to "break the monotony" and provide some food that was different. That very day an old Scotsman gave Harry Ironside a silver dollar. Immediately he went and bought some food—but not beans.

More problems and trials were to come to Harry Ironside in this year. He received word that his mother, Sophia, was very ill. Harry and Helen decided that they would move in with Harry's mother to help care for Lillian, Harry's little half sister. Ironside's mother soon went to be with the Lord. This was a loss that Harry felt deeply.

The following year God blessed Harry and Helen with a son, Edmund Henry. They had already taken five-year-old Lillian to live with them, so now there were two children in the family. But a young Christian couple soon took Harry's stepsister to live in their home.

A short time later, Helen received word that her father had passed away. The Ironsides decided to go home immediately, but they were faced with a serious problem: there was no money for train fare. Shortly before the train was to leave, a friend who had heard of the death of Helen's father gave them money for tickets so they could both go home to attend the funeral.

In 1905 the Lord blessed the Ironside home with another son, John Schofield. Up to this point, Mrs. Ironside had traveled with her evangelist-husband, but now she was confined to her home with the children. More meetings began to come in for Harry Ironside so his traveling and preaching increased.

In addition to his preaching ministry, he also did a great amount of writing, and God blessed his literature ministry richly. The sale of his books was remarkable. He put the money back into more books—giving copies to missionaries, ministers, students, and contributing to the free literature fund of the Western Book and Tract Company, of which he was president. He never accepted any royalties or profits from his writings for himself.

In 1911 another door of witness opened to Mr. Ironside; it was work among the Native Americans. For twelve or more years, he spent two months of each summer with these people in Arizona, southeastern California, and New Mexico. Here he found a receptive people and visited in the native villages and camps of many different tribes.

In 1924 Harry Ironside accepted meetings conducted by the Moody Bible Institute. Before long much of his time was taken up with this work, many of these being Bible conferences from one section of the country to another.

A considerable change had come in the Ironside family life during these years. Edmund entered the Army in World War I, and during this time he married Miss Mabel Guthrie. In 1920 a daughter, Lillian, was born out of this union. But young Mrs. Ironside was quite ill, and shortly after the baby's birth the little girl was taken to be reared by Mr. and Mrs. Harry Ironside. After a time, she was legally adopted by her grandparents. Edmund's wife died of tuberculosis not long afterwards.

Meanwhile, John, who had been a fine Christian, went into a spiritual eclipse in his senior year at the University of California. His doubts as to the reality of spiritual things caused his father and mother much heaviness of heart. Later he and his wife gave themselves over to the Lord and attended and graduated in 1941 from the Moody Bible Institute.

On three different occasions Harry A. Ironside conducted meetings in the well-known Moody Memorial Church in Chicago, the church of which he later became the pastor. The pastor, Dr. P. W. Philpott, had resigned and Mr. Ironside was asked to consider accepting the pastorate of the church. This he did in March 1930.

Dr. Ironside (Wheaton College had now conferred an honorary doctorate degree upon him) continued to be the pastor of the Moody Memorial Church for eighteen years, resigning in 1948. During the time of his pastorate he traveled a great deal, preaching in the United States, Canada, and the British Isles.

Harry A. Ironside, whose very breath was a miracle of God, was used most effectively in preaching, teaching, and writing to men and women throughout the entire world. After resigning from his church, he traveled from country to country, city to city, church to church faithfully preaching the Gospel of Christ. He was the author of more than sixty volumes—many of them pulpit messages, notes, lectures, and expositions of books of the Bible.

Henry (Harry) A. Ironside finally died in Cambridge, New Zealand, in 1951 while on a preaching tour. At his own request he was buried there.

John Knox

John Knox was born at Giffordgate, Scotland. While the exact year of his birth is not known, it is thought to be approximately 1513. Very little is known about his parents other than that his father was the son of a respectable and wealthy landowner, so John was not raised in a poor family. It is assumed from the education John received that his parents were people of intelligence and wealth. Both parents were Catholics.

When John was a very small boy his mother died, and his father married again. When John began college, it was understood that he would become a priest, so he studied Latin and Greek. However, he did not plan to become a priest as far as regular church work was concerned, but rather specialize to become a legal official.

He studied at the University of Glasgow where he spent eight years earning his Master of Arts degree. Immediately upon graduation, he became an instructor of philosophy at the college. At the age of 25, Knox was ordained to the priesthood.

Soon, however, he grew restless with his new position. He was eager to delve deeper into the study of theology. Now he began to see how corrupt the Roman Church in Scotland really was. The more he studied the writings of Jerome and

Augustine, the more they led him into the Scriptures. By resorting to the New Testament and making a critical and thorough study of its truths, his suspicions about the church were confirmed. He made his discovery about 1535, but it took him seven years to decide to renounce the Roman Church and declare himself a reformer.

He knew it would be of little use for him to complain about the corruption he saw in the church. He also knew that if he did say anything he would be considered a heretic and perhaps even be put to death. At the same time, he had to admit that his church was very corrupt. As a result, he began to study and pray and ask God to show him what he should do.

Protestantism was just beginning in the early days of Knox. A preacher by the name of George Wishart began preaching, exposing the evils in the Roman Church. John Knox was so impressed by this man that he learned the truth of the Gospel, left the Roman Church, and followed the work of George Wishart. John became a servant and a helper to the minister and constantly carried a sword to protect him. When Wishart was arrested and condemned to be burned at the stake, he asked Knox to leave him, saying John would no doubt be persecuted and there was no need for both of them to be martyred. Knox argued at first, but finally took the counsel of his friend. However, Knox never saw him again, for Wishart gave his life as a martyr for the Lord Jesus.

Because of his beliefs, Knox was forced to flee from place to place in order to escape arrest. He thought about going to Germany, but his friends persuaded him to take refuge in a castle. So, in the spring of 1547, he did this and took his pupils with him. (He had been a tutor for two families and was partly employed as a priest before this time.) However, knowing he was being sought after, he felt insecure at the castle. Both he and his students soon moved to St. Andrews, where he taught in the chapel every day.

Soon, others came to hear him, and eventually he felt called of God to preach to them. This he did, telling the people of the wickedness of Scotland and the holiness of God.

Now at 40, the once shy Knox suddenly became a bold preacher. He did not try to make beautiful speeches. He told the people that he was a prophet from God and that he did not have good or sweet words, only hard words. With problems and persecutions in the country, Knox continued to show the people their wickedness. He told them that God would send wrath upon them.

The Queen finally ordered that Knox and his followers be carried away by ship to France. There he was sent to the galleys and bound in chains.

One day a painting was brought to the slaves, and they were asked to kiss the painting. John Knox refused, so one of the officers pushed the picture against his face. Rather than kissing the idol, John Knox threw the painting into the water saying "Let our lady now save herself! She is light enough. Let her learn to swim." This he did to show that his heart was with the Protestants in the belief of God and His Son, the Lord Jesus Christ, and not in the Roman Church. While this seems like an unimportant incident, it was from this day on that the other members of the group were no longer required to take part in anything against their own beliefs and were treated with greater respect. After 19 months, Knox was finally released from this ship of slavery. He then went to England, for it was not safe to return to Scotland. Here he found a place in the Protestant English church. Before long he had a good, flourishing congregation.

Now past 40, Knox met Marjorie Bowes with whom he fell in love. Her mother consented to their marriage, but her father refused because of his leanings toward the Church of Rome. After three years of waiting for his consent, they were finally married.

For a time it seemed that everything was going well for John Knox. He did not have the opposition that he had at one time and it seemed that life was a little easier. And this is just the thing that bothered him. He knew that he could not weaken in his form of preaching. He could not ask God to guide him if he was not faithful in proclaiming the truth. Knox determined to be afraid of no one.

In December 1551, he was appointed one of six royal chaplains. As a result, he not only preached at the court of young King Edward VI, who soon became a close friend, but also had outstanding opportunities to visit churches up and down the country. This was very tiring for Knox, but he continued to preach faithfully. Only three years before, he had been a slave on a French ship. Now he was one of the representatives of England, preaching throughout the land, even making suggestions for changes in the order of church service. In July 1553, the young King of England died at the age of 16. The throne was given to Mary Tudor, known in history as "Bloody Mary." It was not long until every law favorable to Protestantism was revoked. Things took a turn for John Knox. His salary was now cut off altogether. His good friends were being martyred.

Knox knew that he could no longer be effective in his ministry in England. He knew he had to leave his wife and her family and flee to France, but he promised to come back. From there he made his way to Switzerland, where he was warmly received by Protestant ministers and churches. After two months he returned to France, glad to find letters waiting for him saying his wife and her mother were safe. But persecution was also on the increase, so it was not safe to return yet.

With a heavy heart he returned to Switzerland. A group of Protestant refugees had formed a church in Frankfurt, Germany and had asked John Knox to become their pastor. He did this for about a year.

In the meantime, political changes had taken place in Scotland. Protestants were allowed more freedom.

By 1555 an urgent appeal was made to him to return to his homeland. He returned by way of England, where he found his wife safe and well. Then he returned to Scotland.

As Knox returned to his country, he noticed that there seemed to be a new spirit in the later generation. He was not only surprised, but, of course, very happy. When John had been in Scotland earlier, he had preached against the Roman Church, the mass, and the tactics used by church leaders. Now he felt that he must preach a more positive message. He still felt that the people should leave the wickedness of the Roman Church, but he had to take them one step further. What could they do when they left that church? He suggested that they celebrate the Lord's Supper every week, that they study the Word, and that they recognize they were part of the Church of Jesus Christ.

Word of his open preaching came to Queen Mary and also to the Scottish bishops. Knowing the type of preacher that Knox was, they summoned him to appear before them on May 15, 1556. But to their surprise, when he appeared in Edinburgh, he was not alone. He had brought with him a large company of people who were ready to take action if anyone did anything to their preacher. Immediately the bishops withdrew their summons, and John Knox was allowed to preach openly and to larger audiences than he had ever preached to before.

Shortly after this he received a call from his church in Switzerland. He returned at once. For the first time, he was able to establish a home in Geneva. During the next three years, two sons were born to Mr. and Mrs. Knox— Nathaniel and Eliezar. Even though he and his family were happily situated in Switzerland, Knox still had a great burden for Scotland. He was again invited by the Scottish Reformed ministers to return to his homeland, and in May 1559 he reached Scotland.

John Knox lost his wife Marjorie in 1560. He was left with the two young children and the care of his mother-in-law. Both sons were given a liberal arts education in preparation for the ministry, but both died early in life and left no children.

All of Knox's life seemed filled with fighting for what he believed—one queen after another, one problem after another, war, strife, and worry; but Knox was determined because he felt he was doing what was right.

Four years after his wife's death, John Knox remarried; this time to Marguerite Stuart Ochiltree, a 17-year-old girl. Knox was 50 and this caused no end of tongue-wagging; but she proved to be a very worthy and congenial mate for Knox, and they lived happily together until his death. From this marriage Knox had three daughters. After his second marriage, he took little part in political or public life. He preached, but quietly.

In the fall of 1570, only a few years after his marriage to Marguerite, Knox had a slight stroke that temporarily afflicted his speech. He couldn't walk or write; everyone thought this was the end. But a week later he was back in the pulpit and preaching again. In November 1572 he again became sick and very weak. His dying day was spent having his wife and others read to him from the Bible. They read for hours, and then, since it was 11 p.m., they knelt to pray. John Knox died peacefully and went to be with the Lord, whom he loved and served.

William Booth

William Booth was not brought up in a Christian home. His father Samuel did not accept Christ as his Saviour until he was on his death bed. But some of the vision that General William Booth had for his work with the Salvation Army was a direct result of seeing the poverty of his own home, as well as that of friends and neighbors.

When William was only 13, his father told him that the family had lost all its money, and the young boy would have to go to work. His father arranged for William to become an apprentice to a pawnbroker, because in that business he could eventually make a great deal of money. The boy tried to tell his father that he was not out to make money; he wanted to help people. But his father did not see the need for this. So while the other boys continued their education, William Booth went to work. His day was not a short one. He often worked from twelve to sixteen hours a day and received but little pay. At night he was so tired he often went to bed without even changing his clothes.

The city of Nottingham, England, where William and his family lived, was a very wicked city. Because of the extremely high taxes, people were very poor. Whenever the men did get money, they went to the saloons and spent almost all of their salary on drink. As a result, the city of

Nottingham produced drunkards by the score. This bothered William a great deal. He knew he had to do something about it. But what could he do?

A group was formed in the city for the express purpose of trying to get people to change the government and improve conditions. When William heard about it, he joined the group, thinking that this was the way he could help. He attended meetings regularly and was faithful in going with the group to get signatures to present to the government. It was not long until he found that there was corruption even within this new organization. Signatures were not always accurate; many of them were forged. Some of them were taken from old city directories and also from gravestones. Instead of having a million signatures as they had thought, they found only about two hundred thousand to be genuine.

Up to this point, William Booth had not accepted Christ as his own personal Saviour. However, when his father was on his death bed, a friend came and told the elderly man about the Lord Jesus. Samuel Booth accepted Christ as his Saviour and died shortly after. Now William began to think more seriously about religious things. He was fifteen years old and began attending the Wesley Chapel in Nottingham. It was there that he accepted the Lord Jesus Christ as his own personal Saviour. Immediately after his conversion, he felt the urge to tell others of the peace that he now enjoyed.

Since William Booth's heart had always been for the poor, it went out even more now that he was a Believer in Christ. One day he brought a group of poor, ragged boys from the slums and took them into the church. Rather than being pleased with the work of William Booth, the minister was very displeased with him. He told William that if he ever again brought in poor people, they must come in through the back door and sit where they would not be seen. This did not discourage Booth. He continued his work with the poorer class of people.

At an early age he began to preach. He soon gave up his work as a pawnbroker and went into the ministry full time. Things were difficult for him, especially since there was no money in preaching. Very often he missed meals and found it very hard to get places to stay, for he could pay very little for his room.

God began to bless the ministry of Booth and especially so when he started his work of evangelism. Rather than staying in one church, he went from place to place preaching the Gospel—sometimes on a street corner, sometimes in an old building, but each time for the glory of God.

By this time the newspapers began to run articles on him and his campaigns. His work even came to the attention of Parliament, where Booth was commended for the work he was doing among the poor.

In one of his services, William met a young lady whose name was Katherine Mumford. Interest developed into love and she became his faithful wife.

After William and Katherine were married, they decided to take a short trip, so they sailed for the Island of Guernsey. When their arrived, they found the pier was filled with people who begged them to conduct revival meetings there. They did, and the crowds were so large and arrived so early the doors of the church had to be opened at 5:30 in order to allow the people to come in for the evening service. Many people came to know Christ as Saviour during this honeymoon-evangelistic meeting. Booth continued his evangelistic meetings with emphasis toward the poor and the drunkards.

By this time the Church Conference decided that Booth should take a pastorate rather than travel as an evangelist. But evangelism was his calling. He tried desperately to explain this to them, but they insisted that he take a church. His work was so effective that the church soon received the title, "the converting shop." In doing house-to-house visitation, Mr. and Mrs. Booth realized more than ever what poverty there was in the city. Families went without food because men used all of their earnings for drink. Finally, Booth told the church leaders that he could no longer be limited to one church, but would have to continue his work of evangelism in order to reach those poverty-stricken people.

Even though they had no means of support, William and Katherine began their new work. It was now that they decided to move to London. By this time there were four children in the family, and with little or no income, things were very difficult for the Booths. Invitations for evangelistic meetings did not come in as quickly as they had thought.

One day William Booth received a sudden invitation to conduct an evangelistic service. The reason it came was that the scheduled evangelist had become ill. A huge tent had been erected on a cemetery lot, and this was in one of the worst locations of the city. Drunkards and tramps made up most of the audience. But as Booth preached the Gospel, many of them came to know Christ as Saviour. The services continued with two meetings every night and four on Sunday. At every service more than a half dozen, and usually up to a dozen people, came forward to accept Christ.

But again finances were a problem because he was preaching to people who had no money, but by faith the Booths continued their ministry. Some of the converts of William Booth's meetings were now beginning to show interest in witnessing for their Saviour. As a result, Booth organized a society to instruct and teach his converts. He also encouraged them to give sacrificially to the Lord's work. He reminded them that when they had bought beer and tobacco, they spent almost all of the money they had, and told them that God deserved nothing less.

Because of the work of William Booth and the testimony of the converts, people from other parts of London asked that meetings be opened in their areas. As new works were started throughout the city, the evangelist always kept in mind that his ministry was with the "worst kind of people." It was his desire to help those who were in need, both spiritually and physically. Most of his converts were uneducated people. They often made mistakes in explaining the Scriptures, but God used their testimonies, and scores of people came to know Christ as Saviour.

By this time there were eight children in the Booth family, and their father prayed that every one of his children would be used in a work similar to his.

One day while William Booth was dictating a letter to his secretary Mr. Railton, he said, "We are a volunteer army." Bramwell Booth heard his father dictating.

"Volunteer," he said, "I'm not a volunteer; I'm a regular." Because of this, William Booth had his secretary cross out the word "volunteer" and write in its place the word "salvation." This was the beginning of the Salvation Army.

Since William Booth was the general superintendent of this work, the title of General was soon given to him. After much prayer and thought, the Booths decided to make the ministry similar to the regular army, using military terms and uniforms. To this day the Salvation Army has continued this policy. Those who are preparing for the ministry with the Salvation Army are known as Cadets, and promotions are given with terms such as Lieutenant, Captain, and General.

Since so many people who were now working with General Booth were able to play instruments, they soon organized a band. This band marched up and down the streets announcing the meetings. When the group settled at a certain corner, the drummer put his drum down in the center. As the service continued and the invitation was given, the drum was used as an altar where people would kneel to accept the Lord as Saviour.

General Booth had a great concern for people who had no place to sleep. One day he asked his oldest son if he knew that there were many people who did not have homes to sleep in.

"Yes," replied the boy.

"Then you ought to have been ashamed of yourself to have known it and done nothing for them," said the general. He instructed his son to go out and find a place where they could bring in some of these people to feed them and provide them with a bed. The young boy did not know what to do, for this would take money. He mentioned this to his father.

"That is your affair," replied General Booth. The boy obediently went out and found an old warehouse. To this day the ministry of the Salvation Army has been to preach the Gospel, to reach men's souls, and to give them food and a place to sleep.

General Booth would often get up from bed at night and pace back and forth in the room. One time when his son asked him what he was doing, he said he was thinking. The boy asked him what he was thinking about. "People's sins," said the father. General Booth still held to the slogan, "Go for souls and go for the worst."

When Katherine Booth was fifty-nine years old, it was discovered that she had cancer. General Booth had already accepted some meetings in Holland, but when he heard of her sickness, he told her he was going to cancel the meetings. She encouraged him to go. "I'm ready to die," she said, "but many of the people over there are not." General William Booth did go to Holland only to come back and find that his wife was very weak. On October 4, 1890, Mrs. William Booth, "Mother" of the Salvation Army, went to be with her Saviour. The streets of London were crowded for four miles as the funeral procession went by. More than ten thousand people went to the cemetery with the family.

After the death of his wife, William continued his work. Shortly after, he sailed to America. The work there was already in progress, for some of the converts had moved from England to the United States. Some five hundred people were active in the Salvation Army work in America. The work grew from country to country, and God blessed it with tremendous increase. General Booth received recognition from the President of the United States, King Edward of Britain, and men of high position in various other countries of the world. As the General continued to age, his eyes became very weak. An operation was performed, but it was not successful. Two days after surgery it was found that he had an infection and that he would lose his sight completely. This also meant that he would be confined to his home.

General William Booth died soon after, finally "laying down his sword," for his work was completed. Sixty-five thousand people marched by as his body lay in state. They wanted to take a last look at the man who had given so much to men who had been counted the outcasts of society.

Charles T. Studd

While the Christian world thinks of Charles T. Studd as an outstanding pioneer missionary, the sports' world remembers him as one of the greatest cricket players England ever produced.

All of the Studds grew up in luxury. Their main interests were hunting, cricket, and their father's racehorses. Because Charles T. Studd came from a very wealthy family, both he and his brothers were able to spend a great deal of time mastering the sport of cricket. At the age of 16, Charles was considered an expert, and by 19, he was made the captain of his team at Eton College.

Charles Studd was a tall, handsome young man who took a great deal of pride in his sports endeavors. He spent many hours before a mirror perfecting his technique.

As a student at Cambridge University, Charles was preparing to go into law practice. But during his senior year, something happened to change all of these plans. As the result of a revival meeting, which was conducted by the outstanding American evangelist, Dwight L. Moody, and his song leader, Ira D. Sankey, Charles' father was genuinely converted. Immediately his time and energies went toward winning others to Christ.

He sold or gave away all his racehorses, except three. Then he emptied the largest room in his beautiful home and invited his friends to attend gospel meetings there. Mr. Studd was attracted to the Moody revival because the papers carried such abusive articles against him. "There must be something good about this man Moody," said Mr. Studd, "or he would never be abused so much by the papers."

After Mr. Studd's conversion, he lived only a short time, but D. L. Moody said that few people had done more for the Lord than he.

One of the things he did was talk to his three sons about their spiritual welfare. However, he was unable to win his son Charles to the Lord.

Later, when his brother George became extremely ill, Charles was deeply moved. For the first time, he realized the real value of spiritual treasures in comparison with worldly possessions. During this time, Dwight L. Moody and Ira D. Sankey were conducting revival meetings in Cambridge. Many of the Cambridge University students attended the services. At first Charles refused to go, for he had never felt any particular need for religion. But he finally attended one of the meetings and was one of hundreds of students who gave their lives completely to Christ. Immediately after this decision, he abandoned his ambitions for a law practice. This disturbed his family a great deal. But Charles insisted that his life now belonged to God and that in the future he would be a missionary.

Charles Studd showed this change in his life by witnessing and testifying of his new faith in Christ. Because he was such a well-known sports' figure, people would come to hear him wherever he went. In this way he was able to witness to many who, otherwise, would not listen to a religious message.

He went to Hudson Taylor, founder of the China Inland Mission, to offer his services as a missionary to China. After having been accepted, he persuaded six of his Cambridge friends to follow in his steps. This group became known as the "Cambridge Seven." The fact that these seven college-trained young men left their businesses and careers and even turned their backs on their wealth created a sensation in the nation. But they had heard God's call, and they were willing to take the Gospel to the unreached millions in China.

In 1885 Charles T. Studd sailed for China to begin his missionary work. Immediately upon arriving in Shanghai on March 18, he began to study and learn the very difficult Chinese language, spending at least seven hours a day in this study.

He, like Hudson Taylor, identified himself with the Chinese by wearing their dress, eating their food, and trying as much as possible to give up his western ways.

While working in that faraway country, Charles received word that his father had died. At this time he also received a letter stating that a large amount of money had been left to him. Because the young missionary had just read the passage from the Bible that said, "Go thy way, sell whatsoever thou hast, and give to the poor, and thou shalt have treasure in heaven," Charles Studd decided to give away much of his inheritance. He gave $25,000 to D. L. Moody, who used it to begin the work of the Moody Bible Institute of Chicago, a Bible-training institution still active today. A similar amount was sent to George Müller to help in his work of taking care of orphans, and a large portion was given to the Salvation Army work in India. Four checks for $5,000 each were also sent to various other Christian leaders.

Three years later after arriving in China, C. T. Studd met and married Pricilla Stewart, a young Irish girl who was also a missionary. God blessed their marriage with five children.

Because the climate in China was not good for Mr. Studd's asthmatic condition, it became necessary for them to return to England. After taking six years to recover, Charles Studd again left for the mission field. This time he went to South India, where the climate was not so severe, and began a church work there. Returning home from this field he was soon challenged with an opportunity to blaze the trail for a work in Africa. He began to work on opening Africa from the Nile to the Niger for Christian missions. On December 15, 1912, he left his wife and four daughters in England and started on his trip to penetrate the heart of Africa. A mission was established at Niangara, and by June 1915 twelve converts were baptized. Studd returned to England to challenge more missionaries, and in 1916 he returned with many fellow workers. The mission was named the World-Wide Evangelization Crusade.

When his wife's health improved somewhat, she took a trip to Africa to see her husband whom she had not seen in years. It was in this country that both Mrs. Studd and the outstanding pioneer missionary, C. T. Studd, died. But because of the World-Wide Evangelization Crusade, his missionary endeavors continued.

Today the Christian world remembers not only the fact that Charles T. Studd was one of the most outstanding cricket players of England, but also that this dedicated young man became a tremendously important worker in God's field of missions.

Martin Luther

Martin Luther, the firstborn child of Hans and Margaret Luther, was born on November 10, 1483, in Eisleben in Saxony, Germany. On the day following his birth, he was dedicated to God; and since that day was St. Martin's Day, Mr. and Mrs. Luther named their son Martin.

The Luthers were very poor and both his father and mother worked hard, not only to feed, clothe, and shelter their children, but also to give them a proper education. There were six other children in the Luther family.

When Martin was only five years old, he began his education. He was sent to the village schoolmaster in Mansfeld where he continued his studies until he was thirteen. Here he was taught not only reading and writing, but also Latin.

At the age of fourteen, Martin began his schooling in the neighboring town of Magdeburg. Since his parents were unable to send him money, Martin had to beg his way through school. This he did for one year. In 1498 he entered the city of Eisenach to attend school. At first, he gained his living by begging, but because of his singing ability, Ursula Cotta, an elderly, wealthy woman, invited him to live in her home. He stayed here for the next four years, finishing his schooling without begging for his meals. Here he learned to play the flute and lute. He often played for Frau Cotta because she had such a love for music.

Luther's adopted mother, Ursula Cotta, loved Luther as her own son and showed him every possible consideration. By Luther's eighteenth birthday his father was financially able to help him in school and sent him to the University of Erfurt. His plans were that Martin be trained in law and follow that profession.

Martin was always a witty, lovable, and talkative companion. His ability to sing and play placed him as a favorite among the students.

Luther received his bachelor's degree in 1502 and ranked thirteen in a class of fifty-seven. In 1505 he received his master's degree, and this time ranked second in a class of seventeen.

One of the greatest events of his life at the University was when he accidentally found a Bible in the library. This he read with great eagerness. While he continued to study law, as was his father's desire, he began to spend much time reading the Bible. He was deeply interested in seeking the truth about God.

Hans and Margaret Luther had always kept very strict discipline in their home. Their children were trained to be afraid of God. From early childhood they were taught the

Creed, the Ten Commandments, the Lord's Prayer, and some hymns and chants.

Children of that day were taught that they had to atone for their own sins; and since they could not make sufficient atonement or do enough good works, they were taught that they would have to call upon the saints in heaven, and upon Mary, the mother of Jesus, to beg Christ to be lenient with them.

It was near the close of his work at the University that a sudden change came over Martin Luther. Because of an accident that almost took his life, and because of the death of a very intimate friend at the University, Martin Luther cried out one day, "Deliver me, St. Ann, and I will become a monk." Even though Luther regretted having made this vow, he felt that since he had made it, he must keep it. He entered the monastery in Erfurt soon after, taking the name of Augustine. He had no intention of turning back, but his friends waited for him outside the monastery gates for two days thinking that he might change his mind. His father was very displeased to think that Martin would leave the law profession to become a monk.

Luther was so eager to obey the three-fold vow of poverty, chastity, and obedience, which he had taken on entering the monastery, that it did not bother him to beg. However, the professors and others at the University saw him and objected to seeing the famous student and popular graduate of their school begging in the streets. They asked the head of the school to put a stop to this, which he did by sending Luther to the country to beg instead of out on the city streets.

In February 1507 Martin Luther was ordained a priest and given a private room in which to study as he pleased. Soon after, he celebrated his first mass. Among the gifts that he received after his first mass was a red leather Bible. This he studied diligently, for he was hungry for the truth. He fasted for many days at a time and went without sleep for nights in order to find the peace that he was seeking, yet no peace came to his soul.

But God was leading! Luther opened his heart to the head of the Augustinian order and told him of his problems and conflicts. One day as they were talking about repentance, the words of his friend convicted Luther. He read the Scriptures until he found that the words spoken by his superior agreed perfectly with what was in the Bible. The thought of repentance no longer brought bitterness to his mind.

In 1508 at the age of 25, because of his unusual work, Martin Luther was made a professor in the newly founded University of Wittenberg. During his three years in the monastery, he had learned both the Greek and Hebrew languages, and as a child had learned the German language at his mother's knee. It has been said that no theologian of that generation received a more careful training than Martin Luther. God was molding a great character for His own use.

Martin Luther's lectures on the Bible were both interesting and enlightening to the people, because for many years no one had been able to read this book except the priests. It was while studying for one of these lectures that Romans 1:17, "The just shall live by faith," stood out to him. Though he was still a priest, he was beginning to learn new truths from the Bible.

Through his studying and searching of the Scriptures, Luther realized that changes in the church were needed. Together with another monk, Martin Luther went to Rome, known as the "Eternal City," on business for the Augustinians.

Upon entering the city after six weeks on foot, he fell to the earth and cried out, "Hail thou sacred Rome," thinking that the city was without sin. Almost as soon as he entered the city, he began hearing and seeing things that grieved and shocked him. While in Rome, he crept up what was known as Pilate's staircase, Scala Sancta, the holy stairway, in order to receive indulgence. On his knees, climbing this stairway, Luther heard a voice within him saying, "The just shall live by faith." This truth became the outstanding doctrine of the Reformation.

Speaking of the city of Rome, Luther later said, "Rome is a harlot. So great and bold is Roman impiety that neither God nor man, neither sin nor shame is feared. All good men who have seen Rome bear witness to this; all bad ones come back worse than before." God had permitted Martin Luther to see the true conditions. As new light was shed upon his soul, Luther did not draw back, nor wait to see where his fellow monks would go; he went onward with Christ.

Luther went back to the University with the text, "The just shall live by faith," burning in his heart. Upon his return, he was made dean of the theological faculty; and the following year, 1512, the University granted him his doctorate in theology. At first, he was hesitant in taking this degree, but later was thankful that he had accepted it, because it gave him the right to teach the Scriptures just as he saw them.

With new zeal Martin Luther took up his duties of teaching. When he was teaching the Book of Romans, he again discovered the doctrine of justification by faith. People attended his lectures in even larger numbers. Here they heard the Word of God proclaimed as they had never heard it before. His teachings were clear.

Luther was not afraid to question the teachings of the church whenever he saw that they were contrary to the Word of God. He began preaching to the monks in an old chapel where the pulpit was made of planks three feet high. Here the Reformation first began.

While studying the Scriptures about the righteousness of God, Martin Luther's own soul was set free. He was made a new man in Christ Jesus, no longer a slave to the Roman Catholic Church and the Pope. The Scriptures looked different to him, and the Bible became more precious each day. It became the center of his preaching and teaching. Of the Bible Dr. Luther said, "What the pasture is to the herd, a house is to a man, a nest is to a bird, a rock is to the chamois, a stream is to the fish, so the Bible is to the faithful soul."

About the same time that Luther experienced his wonderful rebirth by faith, other priests were growing rich by the sale of indulgences. One priest had agents crying out, "Soon as the coin in the chest doth ring, souls out of purgatory spring."

Since Luther knew that men were justified by faith, he could not keep silent. He preached boldly against indulgences. He spoke the truth openly and fearlessly. Many who heard him were troubled, some were annoyed, and others were angered. Eight months later on October 31, 1517, Dr. Luther nailed to the door of his church the now famous "Ninety-Five Theses," a list of propositions concerning indulgences over which he wished to debate. He had preached that justification was by faith. He preached against the priests and the teaching of indulgences. In short, the theses said, "Pardon comes through repentance and the merits of Christ. Indulgences cannot free the soul from the penalty of sin." By nailing these theses on the church door, the spark that started the whole Reformation had begun.

The Protestant Reformation stated that (1) the Bible, not the church, was authority for Christian life; (2) it didn't take money, good works, or anything but faith to become a Christian; (3) all those who believe in Jesus are priests, not just one person.

After clearly stating these views, Dr. Luther found that there were many people of the Catholic faith who had been thinking as he had, but they had been afraid to express themselves. Luther was in danger of being burned at the stake because he had dared to "presume to doubt the Pope's power to forgive sins." Said the Bishop of Brandenburg, "I will not lay my head down in peace until I have thrown Martin into the fire like this brand." Then he threw a piece of wood into the fire.

When the Pope first heard of the theses, he thought they were the writings of some drunken German. He was sure in his heart that whoever had written them would speak differently when he was sober, but gradually one after another of the Pope's own people began to agree with the teachings of Martin Luther.

When the Pope realized that Luther was not a drunken German, but rather a monk and a professor in the University, he sent an order for him to appear in Rome within sixty days to answer to the charges of heresy. Others, who were working with Dr. Luther at the time, assisted him in promising to pay the extreme expenses for the trial to be held in Germany rather than in Rome. Luther appeared before the Cardinal promising only to correct himself if he had in any way misinformed the people. The Cardinal insisted that Luther withdraw the opinions he had set forth. After several unsuccessful meetings, Luther was finally dismissed and told never to show his face to the Pope, unless it was to recant.

The writings of Martin Luther were now in great demand. Words seemed to flow freely from his pen, and he admitted they all but wrote themselves. We know that it was through the guidance of the Holy Spirit that these writings became so great.

In 1520 he wrote several documents that clearly defined his stand against the Roman Church. These rank with the world's greatest documents of history in view of the effects they brought; they changed the whole course of human history.

Luther made clear in both his speaking and writing that the Pope was neither supreme nor infallible. He also made clear that he had found the true Light, the Lord Jesus, and that he had broken with the Church of Rome forever. He stood firmly on his convictions; and as a result, a large body of monks left the monastery where he taught and returned to normal life, giving all of their time and strength to the cause of Christ. Other monasteries followed. Many convents were also deserted when nuns left and returned to normal life.

Several times, Martin Luther was called before church leaders to see if he had not changed his thinking. Each time Luther gave a clear-cut testimony of his faith in the Lord Jesus Christ.

One day Luther was suddenly taken captive, and a heavy coat was thrown over his face so he could not know where he was being taken. This captivity turned out to be an act of mercy. Friends, fearing that his life would be taken by enemies, arranged that he be made prisoner as if by an enemy. He was kept hidden in the old Castle of Wartburg. Only the keeper of the Castle knew his true identity; the inmates thought he was a knight, for he dressed in a disguise. The world in general thought he had been killed.

This captivity was, no doubt, ordained of God, for here Martin Luther had much time to think and write. He was not only a master of the German language, but also of Latin, Greek, and Hebrew. He translated the entire New Testament into the German language in less than three months, and soon after, it was in the hands of the people. From the Castle of Wartburg, he continued his translation work on the Old Testament. But it was not until after he had returned to Wittenberg that the entire Bible in the German language came from the press.

About a year later, Luther returned to Wittenberg where he was badly needed. Immediately on his return, he stepped back into his old place as leader. He again set the people straight in their thinking. He gave the Bible answers for every question.

Marriage, which had been heretofore forbidden, now became a common practice with nuns and priests. After some time and consideration, Dr. Luther laid aside his monk's attire, rejected the title of monk, and on June 13, 1525, married Catherine von Bora, a former nun. On the wedding rings of both Martin and Catherine Luther was the inscription: "What God hath joined together, let no man put asunder."

He and his bride set up housekeeping in the Augustinian cloister from which almost all the monks had fled. God blessed this marriage with six children. One of Luther's sons, Hans, studied law; another son, Paul, became a doctor. Martin Luther's earnest desire was that one of his children should follow in his footsteps, but his son, Martin, who began to study theology, died before he finished his studies.

Marriage softened and mellowed the reformer. As a husband and father his character reached its finest proportions.

While the Reformation has always been considered the greatest work of Luther's life, he also has many great writings. Music was also a highlight in his life. During the hard, trying years when the Reformation was first started, he wrote the well-known song, "A Mighty Fortress Is Our God." He not only wrote many hymns, but also compiled the first hymnbook and introduced congregational singing in the church services. Until Luther's time, there were no hymnbooks and the congregation did not take part in singing.

Luther also organized a system of church visitation whereby the new churches were visited from time to time and helped by some able leader. He drew up a set of instructions to serve as a guide to the local pastors. When he saw the need of an order of service, he wrote it out fully and added it to the hymnbooks which were already in use.

He made the sermon the very heart and core of the public worship service.

Dr. Martin Luther has often been called "the father of public schools." It was he who first realized that unless the common people, the peasants, were taught to read, they would always be handicapped in their spiritual growth. He outlined a course of study to be followed in training the young people of his day. His influence was great in the establishment of schools for the common people.

In 1527 Luther became ill and thought that he would soon die; however, he did not. He continued to work for the Lord until 1546. That year he took a journey in the winter (January 23) even though he was not well. Arriving at Eisleben, he became much worse. In spite of this, he preached four times, administered the Lord's Supper twice, and ordained two ministers. By February his illness had become much worse. Luther was sure his time was now very short.

"Do you die firm in the faith you have taught?" he was asked on his death bed. "Yes," he answered. Between two and three o'clock in the morning, February 18, 1546, he went to be with the Lord Jesus whom he learned to love so dearly.

Dr. Martin Luther, a great and courageous man of God, had died; but his work and influence continues to live on today through the Protestant faith and active ministry of winning men and women to Christ and bringing them from darkness to light.

John G. Paton

There were 11 children in the family to which John Gibson Paton was born. They lived in a beautiful Scottish village, though their home was a very humble one. John's father had a workshop where he manufactured stockings. Before John was twelve years of age, he left school and started to work at home, learning his father's trade. Although he was employed at home, his working hours were just as long as those in the factories. Like his father, John sat at his machine from six in the morning until ten at night.

From the time John Paton accepted Christ as his Saviour, he had one main ambition—to be a missionary. He knew this would mean a great deal of studying and learning, so he spent much time poring over his books. After some time he had saved enough money from his earnings to go away to school.

While he was a student at Dumfries Academy, John decided to give up his father's trade and look for a job that would leave him more time to study. One day he was offered a very fine government job. He was told that he would get a promotion if he would promise to stay with the group for at least seven years. They even offered to pay him while he took a special course of study. It was a very tempting offer, but seven years seemed so long and John knew that he must go to the mission field.

"I will promise to stay three or four years," he said.

The director of the government job asked, "Why? Why only three or four years?"

"Because I have given my life to another Master," replied John.

"To whom?"

"To the Lord Jesus. I want to prepare to serve Him as soon as possible."

This made the employer so angry that he dismissed John Paton from his job immediately. When the principal of the school where John attended heard of this, he permitted the young man to study without paying the fee. Since he had no income while he studied, he decided not to take advantage of this kind offer. Instead he went to work for a farmer for a few months to help in the harvesting. Later, John returned to school, but because of broken health, he was again forced to leave.

As soon as he felt able to work again, he rented a house and started a school, but he kept hoping he would be able to return to college to finish his studies. When he had saved enough money he did go back, but his money was all spent before he finished the course. This was because he had loaned some of it to a poorer student who couldn't repay him. Once more John Paton had to leave.

Again he taught school—this time a church school. The attendance grew until the school was overcrowded. It gained such a good name that it was decided to appoint a more highly trained teacher.

As soon as he left this school, he was invited to become a missionary of the Glasgow City Mission. He gladly accepted, and for the next ten years worked among people living in some of the city's worst slums. During this time he was also in charge of a church. All of this was good preparation for his missionary work in the Pacific Islands. In March 1858 John was ordained a missionary, and a few weeks later he and his bride, Mary Ann Robson, left for the New Hebrides.

After a long and tiring journey, Mr. and Mrs. Paton finally arrived at Tanna, an island inhabited by savage cannibals. Here they were to begin their ministry of missions and these young missionaries did not ask to be excused. They knew that the place of greatest danger was also the place of greatest need. They had volunteered for this work because God had called them to it.

John's first job was to learn the language. Listening to the men speak, and asking many questions, he learned the names of various objects and eventually learned the language. Then his desire was to translate the Bible into the language of the people and teach the Tannese to read.

But everything did not go well for John Paton. Within a short time his wife died of malaria and two weeks later their baby boy also died. This made Paton a very lonely man, but he knew God had sent him to the New Hebrides, and he could not forget his ministry.

Very often Paton's life was in danger. Various tribes in the area determined to kill him. Whenever there was a death in the village the people blamed the missionary.

"It is your God," they said. "We must kill you."

Two of the most common problems in the area were stealing and lying. The natives took anything they wanted even though it belonged to Paton. When they were caught, they would deny their act and refuse to return the item. Because of this, he lost much of the equipment he had brought with him.

John G. Paton's missionary life was one of danger and difficulties. His life was continually threatened. Even the people who seemed to be his friends would turn on him from time to time. After four years of preaching and suffering, Paton returned to Scotland for a brief furlough. He spent all of his time telling the people of the needs of the mission field, urging young men to go as missionaries and others to contribute to the work. The result of his pleading for workers was that four young men offered themselves for missionary work in the New Hebrides.

When he was ready to return to the islands again in January 1865 he did not go alone, for in the meantime he had married Margaret Whitecross.

Mr. and Mrs. Paton picked up their work in the New Hebrides on Aniwa, a small island near Tanna, and again they found dangers and difficulties facing them. Here Paton had to learn a new language, but he found that the methods used in Tanna were equally successful here. A few of the people could understand Tannese, and with their help he made rapid progress.

With God's help they slowly won the confidence of the people and continued their ministry until converts were made in various parts of the islands. But enemies continued to hinder the work, and so did the elements. A tropical hurricane pulled up trees and demolished huts, so Paton's work of building began all over again.

Another desperate need was for fresh water for drinking and washing. Paton began digging a hole, telling the people that he would finally reach water. They laughed, thinking he had lost his mind. "Rain comes from the sky," they said. But Paton continued to dig. After much effort he finally came to an area that was damp. He knew that the next day he would reach water, so he called the people together and asked them to watch as he produced water from the earth.

"Rain out of the ground!" the people said. "How did you get it?" John told them that God had given it in answer to prayer. The well did more to break heathenism on Aniwa than much preaching. Later, when there had been no rain for a long time, it was this well that saved the people from dying of thirst.

After some time of meeting with the converts in their homes, John Paton encouraged them to build a church. These Christians were enthusiastic and began to work on the building. However, as soon as the building was finished, a hurricane came to the island and completely destroyed the church. At first the people were very discouraged, but finally their chief said, "Let us not weep like little boys over broken bows and arrows, but let us build another and stronger church for God." Once more the people joined their efforts and produced a bigger and better church and dedicated it exclusively for the worship of God. Paton held his first communion in 1869 in the new house of worship. He then gave to the Aniwan people the first hymnbook in their own language.

Mr. and Mrs. Paton also built two orphanages, one for boys and the other for girls. Many of these young people later became evangelists and teachers, taking the Gospel to their own villages.

On January 28, 1907, at the age of eighty-three, John G. Paton finished his work on earth. But other missionaries went to take his place, among them one of his sons, Frank. When the people saw these new missionaries come, they said, "How is this? We drove the missionaries away. We tore down their houses and robbed them. If we had been treated like this we would never have returned. But these people came back to tell us of Jesus. If their God makes them do all these things, we must worship Him too."

So John G. Paton's work continued in the New Hebrides Islands even though his life had come to an end.

Adoniram Judson

Even though Adoniram Judson was brought up in a strict minister's home, he did not give his heart and life to Christ until he was a young man.

"Don" was a very bright boy. When he was only three years old, he could read and recite an entire chapter from the family Bible. When his father noticed this, he sent him away to give him the very best education that was possible. At the age of twelve Judson had mastered Greek, a very difficult language to learn.

Adoniram Judson had never been sick or at least not seriously sick; but when he was fourteen, he became very ill and thought he might die. While lying in bed, he began to think more seriously than ever before. If he followed the Lord Jesus, he would have to give up all his plans for becoming a great person. He had to be honest with himself—if that was what it meant to be a Christian, he didn't want to be one. So as soon as he was better, it was easy to forget his thoughts about becoming a Christian.

By the time Judson was sixteen, he enrolled at Brown University. Through the urging and influence of another student, Adoniram Judson developed many questions in his mind about a belief in God. By the time he finished his studies, he had almost no belief in God at all. Upon completion of his college work, Judson went home for a while before starting on a tour of the northern states. He found it very hard to explain to his father how his ideas had changed. His father had expected him to follow in his footsteps and become a minister. Mr. Judson tried to argue his son out of these new ideas, but he was not successful. Adoniram could see how deeply hurt his parents were to think that their son was an unbeliever, but even this did not change him. He left on his tour, saddened by the division that had come between his family and him, and shaken at the thought of the kind of life he had chosen to live.

For about a year after his work at the University, Judson traveled with a theatrical group, all the time feeling somewhat uncomfortable. Somehow his dreams of becoming someone great seemed to turn into something shabby. Finally he got on his horse and began to travel with no definite plans in mind.

One night he stopped for a room at an inn. The man at the desk told him there was only one room left, but that it was quite a noisy room. He explained that the room next to the vacant one was occupied by a young man who was very sick—perhaps even dying.

This did not seem to bother Adoniram Judson very much. He was sure he was so tired that nothing would keep him from sleeping, but that night he found things quite different. He heard every noise in the room—the footsteps of the doctor, as well as the moans and groans of the sick man. Judson found it very hard to sleep. His mind kept going back to the thought: "Is he ready to die?" Perhaps the man in the next room was an unbeliever like himself.

The next morning Adoniram Judson was still tired.

"How did you sleep?" asked the clerk of the inn.

Judson had to admit that he had hardly slept at all. The hotel manager told Judson that the young man next door had died during the night.

"He was about your age," said the innkeeper. "Went to Brown University back East."

Brown University. That was the school Judson had attended. He wondered if he knew the man and asked for his name. The clerk gave Adoniram Judson the name of the young man, and Judson found it was the same man who had had no use for God, and who had influenced his thinking in the same way.

Now he knew his life had been wrong. Quickly he turned his horse around and headed for home. Immediately he decided that he would study for the ministry, but there was still something wrong. He had not yet given his heart and life to the Lord Jesus. Three months later, and after studying both the Old and New Testaments, he did give himself to Christ. Six months later he joined the church where his father was the pastor.

Even now he was not as happy as he felt he should be. Somehow, he felt there was something he must do for God. Then he found it. It all started when he began reading a book written by a chaplain to the East India Company. Judson was fascinated as he read about the people of India and the false gods that they worshiped. The book showed how the Gospel and the love of Jesus Christ had brought light to people there. Suddenly he felt a sincere longing to share in the work that was being done.

One day while walking through the woods, he talked with God and asked Him what he should do with his life. All at once a Bible verse came to him: "Go ye into all the world, and preach the gospel to every creature." God seemed to tell him to go to India. He knew that the Lord was calling him to help preach the Gospel, so he gave his life fully to the Lord for His service. Soon after this, he met and married Ann Hasseltine, a wonderful Christian girl. Together Mr. and Mrs. Judson planned their trip to India. Neighbors thought it was wrong for Adoniram Judson to take his bride to a country such as India, but Ann was very willing to go. She, too, felt that God was leading them there. This would be something different and dangerous, for she would be the first woman in America to choose such a career. On February 19, 1812, Adoniram and Ann Judson watched America's shores fade into the distance as they set out into an unknown future.

The trip was long, tiring, and hard, but after an exciting voyage of four months, Mr. and Mrs. Judson finally arrived in Calcutta, India. They were not there long, for just a short time after they arrived they were forced to leave the country in the middle of the night. The East India Company announced that they wanted no missionaries there. After many stormy voyages, the Judsons finally arrived in Rangoon, a large city in Burma.

In Burma, Judson saw many nationals who needed the Lord Jesus as Saviour. He soon found that even though the country was wealthy and beautiful, it was a land made up of mixed tribes and strange religions. The only buildings of any size or beauty were the great pagodas—temples of Buddhism, the national religion.

One of the strange customs of this country was the belief that the white elephant was a sacred animal. Whenever one was captured, the people would lead it right into the king's court. Here, the huge animal was allowed to go any place on the royal grounds.

The Buddhist worshipers also believed that the souls of men were born time and time again in different physical forms. If they had kept the rules of their religion, they would move higher up the scale of living creatures—but even then, each new life had to have a time of suffering and trial. The only way to escape from the evil of being born again and again into this world of evil, pain, sickness, and death, was to reach "Nirvana," which means "nothingness."

In working with these people the Judsons found that they did not live up to the law that had been laid down by Buddha. They had nothing to look forward to but to go on and on in this cycle of dying and being born. It was no wonder the young missionaries longed to tell them the glad news of the Gospel.

Adoniram began at once to work on learning the language. Ann took on the management of the house so that her husband could be free to concentrate on his studies, but all this time she was picking up the language too—almost more quickly than he. Neither of them, however, found it easy to learn Burmese.

After Mr. and Mrs. Judson had been in Burma for a time, God gave them a little baby boy. They named him Roger William. He was a happy little baby for a time, but because of the climate in Burma, at eight months, the child became sick and died. Mr. and Mrs. Judson were very sad, but at the same time, they knew that their son was with the Lord.

Soon after this, Judson also became sick. Long hours of study month after month would have been bad enough in that hot climate, but the "books" of the Burmese were only dried palm leaves strung together, the letters poorly scratched on them. It was no wonder that Judson complained of eyestrain and headaches. For months he lay in bed, his eyes sore from disease.

During the time of his sickness, he began working on a grammar book of the Burmese-English language. He also wrote a gospel tract telling of salvation in the Lord Jesus Christ.

Soon thrilling news came. A missionary couple was coming to share their work. They were Mr. Hough, a missionary printer, and his wife. The news was like a tonic to Adoniram. He soon felt much better and was able to get on with his study again.

One day, after talking with a man who wanted to know about "the Jesus religion," Adoniram Judson decided that he must translate the Bible into the language of the people. Before he could do this, he would have to make a dictionary so he could learn all the words in this new language. This he did. Now Judson felt the time had come to start preaching the Gospel in public. He had kept very quiet until now, studying and translating, though he had always been ready to answer all the questions of those who came to him.

Judson found that in order to make friends with the Burmese people, he would have to make a "zayat" for them to use. A zayat was a large public building where the farmers and business men gathered to talk and relax at any time of the night or day. Finding a spot on one of the busy roads, Mr. Judson soon made the zayat. When the travelers found that the white man had not put up this building for money, and that they were able to stay here without paying, they soon became very friendly toward the missionaries.

Mr. Judson's first Christian service in the Burmese language was held in the zayat on April 4, 1819. Fifteen adults and many children came to the meeting. There was much disorder and inattention because the Burmese were not used to Christian worship, but every native who stopped at the zayat was told God's way of salvation. Many of them admitted that the Christian religion was "interesting" and promised to stop again to hear more.

About this time a new king had come into power. Unlike the one who had just died, he was devoted to the national religion of Buddhism. As a result, a new interest was shown in the pagodas. Hundreds of Burmese made regular offerings in the temples of Buddha. New pagodas were built and the old ones repaired. Judson's zayat was now shunned by the Burmese. To show an interest in the foreigner's religion was to put one's life in danger.

Although Judson now had to carry on his work quietly and be careful not to let it be known who was inquiring about the Christian religion, he found that the church was growing steadily.

After three or four years had passed, bad news came again. The English had captured the city of Rangoon. The king and his officers, horrified at this unexpected victory, looked around for someone to blame. Who else could it be but the "English" missionaries?

One day a band of soldiers rushed into the missionaries' home, saying, "You are wanted by the king." This was another way of saying, "You are under arrest." In Burma all foreigners were thought of as spies, so Mr. Judson was taken away and put in prison. Nothing Ann Judson could say, no offer of money she made, could prevent them from dragging him away.

Judson spent many months of near starvation in prison. His clothes were torn from his body and his arms were tied behind him. For some days Ann remained more or less a prisoner herself, and it was only after repeated pleas to the governor of the city, who was also in charge of the prisons, that she was able to get permission to visit Adoniram. She would take some food for him and the other prisoners and bring in mats for them to lie on.

Time after time Adoniram Judson and some of the other prisoners were led to the execution chamber, but each time Mr. Judson's life was spared. He knew that God was protecting his life so that he could preach the Gospel to more of these people.

Finally after repeated interviews with the governor and after many gifts of money, Ann Judson managed to get her husband released from the death prison and brought out into the courtyard of the jail, where there was an open shed. Anything was better than the conditions inside.

Because Judson was a prisoner of the crown, an official was sent to his house to take away all the property. Ann managed to hide some of her personal belongings and a little money. She took her husband's translation of the New Testament and carefully wrapped it and buried it in the garden. Later she dug it up, sewed it in a pillow, and smuggled it to him in the prison.

Things continued to get worse now for Adoniram and his fellow prisoners. Ann was unable to visit them for several weeks, for their little daughter, Maria, was born at this time, and she was busy taking care of her. When she was able to go and see them again, she found that they had been put back into the death prison. Here Judson became very ill with a high fever and only managed to stay alive because of Ann's constant care and nursing.

All the time that Adoniram Judson was in prison, his wife continued to share the Gospel. Each day she walked to the royal palace and begged the men to let her husband go.

She tried to explain that they were American missionaries and that they had come to Burma to present the Gospel and not to spy on the government. But each time she was given the same answer, "It makes no difference whether you are American or English. All foreigners must be treated as enemies."

Then one day the English army drew near. The Burmese jailors became so frightened that they quickly released all the prisoners. Immediately after this release, Mr. and Mrs. Judson left for other parts of Burma and there continued their missionary work. He settled his family in Amherst, a new British settlement, and then returned to Ava. While he was gone, Ann caught a fever and died. She was only thirty-seven. His little daughter died three months after he returned, and he was left without a family or a home.

Amherst was not a good place from which to reach the people of Burma with the Gospel, so shortly after Ann's death Judson moved to another town. Here he and another missionary opened zayats in the town and found many inquirers with a real interest in the Gospel. The first year there, Judson and his fellow missionary saw thirty Burmese converts baptized and received into the church.

In April 1834 he married Sarah Boardman, the widow of a missionary friend who had died while on a preaching tour. One year later God blessed them with a little daughter.

Judson named her "Abbie" after his own sister, who had held such a high place in his heart. Three years later they had a little boy, Adoniram, and then another son, Elnathan, named after his uncle.

As years went by, the Burmese church membership increased to some 160 members. Judson would preach and teach all morning in the zayat and then in the evening would hold a service for Believers and inquirers. But he was finding it more difficult to speak in public. He had been ill so many times that his lungs and throat were affected. His voice was growing weak.

Mrs. Judson was repeatedly ill, and Adoniram soon realized she would have to return to America for a time. She was too sick to go alone, so he decided to take her. But Mrs. Judson never regained her health and died in the port of St. Helena. She never saw her native land again.

After thirty-two years of hard work on the field, Judson returned to America for a furlough. Much to his surprise, a railroad system had spread over the nation. How good it was to travel on the train rather than by oxcart or horseback as they had in Burma.

Once again Judson longed to return to Burma. A month before he sailed, he married for the third time. Emily was a gifted writer. Upon arrival, they found that the reigning king was strongly against Christianity. Judson spent much time working on his dictionary, as he was not allowed to do much else.

In November of 1849 he caught a bad cold, which was followed by a severe attack of the fever he had several times before. On board ship to Mauritius, the great pioneer of American missionary work spent his last hours. He was buried at sea just three days out of sight of the mountains of Burma, the land to which he had dedicated his life.

The work of Adoniram Judson has never been forgotten, for missionaries today are walking many of the trails that were first paved by him.

Though the trials and testings were great, God took care of this man, and, as a result, thousands of people in Burma today are Christians.

John Wesley

It was on June 17, 1703, that John Wesley was born into the home of a minister's family; he was the fifteenth child. Not only was his father a minister, but his grandfather and great-grandfather had been ministers too.

All of the Wesley children were well-behaved and well-educated, although they were desperately poor. Their mother was their school teacher. She taught them the regular school subjects and gave them excellent Christian training as well. Each of the girls in the Wesley family learned Greek, Latin, and French, as well as lessons in homemaking. The children were taught a delightful courtesy, very unusual in those days, toward each other and toward their servants and neighbors.

In spite of the fact that Susanna Wesley was a very busy mother, she made it a point to take each of her children aside on his fifth birthday and teach him the alphabet. In each case she was successful.

One day when John Wesley was only six, the old parsonage caught fire. As the house was burning, every member of the family escaped except young John. His father was just about to run back into the house to look for the young child when it appeared that the entire house was about to collapse. All this time John had been sleeping, but when one side of the house fell, the loud crash awakened him and brought him running to a window. Since there was no ladder anywhere nearby, one neighbor jumped on the shoulder of another and they were able to rescue the young boy just as the roof fell in. This experience was long remembered by John Wesley, and he felt that God had spared his life for a specific purpose.

Mrs. Wesley tried to spend some time each week with each of her children. She also found time, or made time, to talk to each of them about God and about praying to Him and pleasing Him. Thursday evening became the night she spent with young John. This made a deep impression on him, something he remembered even when he went away to Oxford University. He would often write his mother, reminding her to think about him on Thursday evenings.

When John was ten years old, his father took him to Charterhouse School in London. Here he received a sound education, one of the best that could be had anywhere in the land in that day. He studied the classical languages, mathematics, and science.

When, at the age of seventeen, John left Charterhouse, he went to Oxford University. For the first time he became his own master. In spite of the fact that he was thrown in with other students, some who drank, gambled, and lived immoral lives, he proved what his Christian home training had done and thereby lived a good, clean life.

Wesley made many friends during this time at the University. He had a quick humor and a unique gift of writing poetry. He was the life of any party at which he found himself and was always welcome in the homes of some of his fellow students who lived in nearby villages.

Following in the footsteps of his great-grandfather, his grandfather, and his father, John Wesley decided to become a minister. He preached his first sermon in a small church in a village called South Leigh.

After Wesley had obtained his bachelor's degree, and after he had spent some time helping his father in Lincolnshire, he was appointed Fellow of Lincoln College, a position he held with honor to himself and the College for 25 years.

It was at that time that John Wesley began to develop into a High Churchman, believing in all the forms and ceremonies of the established church, and also in severe discipline. He got up at four o'clock, fasted regularly, worked hard every minute, and strained his strong body almost to the breaking point. He visited the prisoners in the jail (prisons were terrible places in those days). He tried to brighten the lives of the inmates wherever he went, and he taught children who had nobody to look after them. Despite all this tireless religious activity and his preaching of carefully prepared sermons, he could not help but feel that his life was a fruitless one. He drew no crowds. He influenced no lives. He touched no consciences. He warmed no hearts.

After a time, Wesley's young brother, Charles, went up to Oxford and, with some other of the more serious-minded students, formed a group that some called "The Holy Club." They met to pray, study the Bible, and talk over what they had been reading and thinking. They were very regular in their attendance at communion services, and, because of all these practices, students began to call them "Methodists."

In October 1735 John and Charles Wesley went to America. John was to serve as chaplain in Savannah, Georgia, while Charles had the position of secretary to the founder and governor, General Oglethorpe. John arranged a number of services, visited every home, and organized schools for the settlers' children. He tried to teach the Native Americans, but they did not welcome his efforts in the least.

He was tremendously busy, not at all popular, and all the time in the back of his mind he was searching for a true belief in God.

Meanwhile, Charles Wesley had managed to work up a big quarrel with the governor, and as a result returned to

England. After less than two years in Georgia, John followed his brother back to England. The Georgia adventure, which began with such high hopes, was a bitter disappointment.

Both John and Charles Wesley had made professions of their faith in Christ, but neither one felt that he was out-and-out for the Lord. Again and again John read the story of Paul's conversion and prayed that he, too, might have a blinding flash and an assured belief that he was an accepted servant of Christ his Saviour. It was this that led to a search on the part of both young men, and it was this that brought a complete assurance of their faith in Christ.

From that day on, things were different for John Wesley. He wanted more than anything to share this conversion experience with other people who did not seem to have real joy in the Lord. Immediately he tried to preach in some of the established churches of England. People flocked in great crowds to hear him. The message he gave was so simple, so direct, and so convincing that men and women who felt the burden of their sinful lives cried out in repentance.

But other clergymen would not accept his message. Before long he found he had to get his own places to speak—in the open air. This he did and hundreds of people still gathered to hear the message of John Wesley.

Now he began his ministry on horseback, traveling up and down the roads of England to preach the Gospel of Christ to the people. He was fit and fearless. He preached in any building, large or small, that was available. When there was none to be had, he preached out of doors in any spot where people could gather. He was always willing to preach, even to one person. When he was riding alone, he rode with a slack rein so that he could read. That was how he kept up his wide studies and made his many sermons.

Still not being able to get into the regular parish churches, Wesley decided to build preaching houses in the various places where he visited. By designing these buildings so that they could be used either as schoolrooms or churches, he was able to help neglected and uneducated children as well. In some of the preaching houses he also built rooms that could be used by traveling evangelists who had no place to go for the night. There was also a stable for a couple of horses.

Every place he went, hundreds and sometimes thousands would gather to hear him speak. John Wesley realized that he could not continue this big work by himself, so he began to use the services of lay preachers. These were men who preached on Sunday and continued their regular jobs during the week. They were poorly paid, poorly clad, poorly equipped, and poorly housed, but they had the courage of heroes. They covered vast distances, mostly on horseback, sometimes even on foot. They faced bitter persecution. They were often scolded by officials and sometimes imprisoned.

Wesley had a particular interest in children and young people and would often go into a town and visit with them before starting his meetings. He never tired of telling them, as he told the adults, that what they had to do was "to believe, to love, and to obey." It was because of this interest that he was later able to provide homes, schools, and church services for these young people.

There were few people in England who were rich. There were many who lived comfortably but a very large part of the population was either unemployed or underpaid and desperately poor. They lived in unsanitary homes, and their children were underfed, ill clad, and for the most part uneducated. John Wesley never turned a deaf ear or a blind eye to the needs of those who were less fortunate than he. He lived sparingly so that he could give more to the needy.

As Wesley's work widened, he arranged for others to carry on the activities for people who needed sympathy and help. He started orphanages where children were cared for and educated. He also managed to find rooms for elderly women and arranged care for them. He started a public dispensary and actually distributed medicines himself. Gifts of money, clothing, food, and fuel were collected from the more prosperous Methodists and taken to the homes of those who were sick or desperately poor.

Mr. Wesley's ministry was not limited to England. It also took him to Ireland, America, Canada, and the West Indies. In each place large crowds came to hear him.

Because he saw the value of literature and because he was a scholar, John Wesley wrote nearly 300 books and pamphlets on various subjects: theology, history, logic, science, medicine, and music. He wrote many devotional books, which he distributed to the people he met. These were published in inexpensive forms, giving the people an opportunity to buy them. This work grew so rapidly that Wesley finally set up his own publishing house. Here, also, hundreds of songs were printed—many of them written by his brother Charles.

On March 2, 1791, at the age of 88, John Wesley's lifework came to a close. Yet what he began has continued through the Methodist church for over 200 years. God blessed the life and ministry of this dedicated saint who had only one desire—to preach the Gospel of Christ, encouraging people to believe, love, and obey.

Billy Sunday

William Ashley Sunday was born in Iowa on November 19, 1862, to pioneer parents whose home was a two-room log cabin. Billy was born four months after his father left for military service. Mrs. Sunday named her third son after her soldier husband, hoping he would soon come home to see the young boy. But within four months she received word that Pvt. William Sunday had contracted a disease and died in Patterson, Missouri.

Billy spent much of his boyhood on the farm belonging to his grandfather, Squire Martin Corey. He didn't like farm life and from his youth planned to make his living by other means. He once told his grandfather, "I'm going to hunt around and find a good job I can do with my head."

For several years his mother held the home together, but finally she had to decide to send two of the boys to an orphanage. Ed and Billy were sent to the Soldiers Orphans Home at Glenwood, Iowa. They did not have money for train fare, so they crawled into a freight car. When the conductor asked them for their tickets they said, "We ain't got any." The conductor told them he would have to put them off, but when the boys explained that they were on their way to the orphans' home, he let them ride without charge.

A year and a half later that home closed, and they were sent to the Orphans Home at Davenport, Iowa. This home had a strong religious influence, and there Billy was taught to believe in the divine authority of the Bible. Although he did not accept Christ until later in his life, he had a good knowledge of the Bible and mentally believed it as a result of the years in this home.

Billy Sunday did not have a great deal of education though he did go to school off and on. He began working for a living when he was fourteen years old. This job was that of a janitor in a school. He carried coal and filled fourteen different stoves in the school. His salary was twenty-five dollars a month.

At 15, he and Ed left the home and went to live with their grandfather Corey. This man practically became a father to the boys. Once when Billy wanted a white, store collar to wear to a spelling bee, his grandfather told him that if he was honest and worked hard, he wouldn't need a collar to make people look up to him. Remembering this years later, Billy said in a youth meeting, "It is not what you have on you but what you have in you that makes you a man."

He soon wearied of farm life and rented a horse and went to a nearby town. For eight months he worked as a bellboy and janitor at a cheap hotel, sleeping behind the counter. His only pay was this and his board.

Later he became an errand boy for Colonel Scott. His thoroughness and enthusiasm at little tasks won him the job. At this time he established himself as a runner. He became one of the first men in the country to run 100 yards in 10 seconds.

After he finished high school, Billy got a job in Marshalltown, Iowa, so he could join the fire brigade there. His fleetness of foot won him acclaim at the job. It was during this time that he began to play on the local baseball team.

One day when Billy Sunday was twenty years old, he was playing baseball in one of the lots in Marshalltown. While there, a famous leader of the Chicago White Stockings (later named White Sox) saw him and signed him up to play ball. He began his professional career in 1883. Billy Sunday became one of the fastest base runners and most daring base stealers on the team, and his name became very well known to those who enjoyed baseball. For five years he played with the Chicago team, usually in either the right or center field position. Later he signed with Pittsburgh and Philadelphia but, after eight years of baseball, refused to sign another contract (although the salary offered him was $500 a month). He refused so that he could go into Christian work. Billy Sunday had accepted Christ as his personal Saviour in 1887, four years after he began his baseball career. The men on the team knew him as a Christian—an out-and-out Christian. Because of his religious beliefs, Billy refused to play baseball on Sunday.

One day while Billy Sunday was preaching, a man from the Cincinnati team came up on the platform, pulled out a contract, and asked the evangelist to sign. He offered him $3,500 for the seven months of playing and also agreed to give him $500 in advance. But Billy said, "No." He told the Cincinnati man how God had called him to preach.

How was Billy Sunday saved? It was through the ministry of the Pacific Garden Mission in Chicago and the direct ministry of a Mrs. Clark. Billy and five of his baseball teammates were walking down a street in Chicago. It was a Sunday afternoon and in Billy Sunday's own words, "We got tanked up and then went and sat down on a corner." Across the street from where the six men were sitting, a group of men and women were playing instruments and singing gospel hymns. It reminded Billy of the songs his mother used to sing back in Iowa. A young man from the Pacific Garden Mission came over to where the baseball players were seated. "We are going to the Pacific Garden Mission. Won't you come down to the service?" he asked.

Billy Sunday was deeply touched by the singing of the hymns. He turned to his fellow players and said, "I'm through; I'm going to Jesus Christ." Some of them laughed at him; others encouraged him. It was that night that Billy Sunday fell on his knees and accepted Jesus Christ as his personal Saviour. Instead of finding that the ball players made fun of him, he found there was respect. Mike Kelly, a teammate, said, "Bill, I'm proud of you. Religion ain't my long suit, but I'll help you all I can."

Immediately after Billy Sunday's conversion, he began to associate himself with the Jefferson Park Presbyterian Church in Chicago. He attended the Christian Endeavor Society, the prayer meetings, and the midweek services. It was at this church that he met Helen Thompson, who later became his wife. Even though Miss Thompson's parents did not think she should marry a professional baseball player, the young couple was married in September 1888, and their wedding trip was going on the circuit with the baseball team.

After leaving baseball, Billy Sunday joined the YMCA, not as a physical director but to help in the spiritual aspect of the work. One of his duties was to find a speaker for the noonday prayer meetings. Other jobs were raising money, distributing literature, and taking care of office work.

Billy's ministry at the YMCA also included reaching many of the men who were penniless because of drink. He helped many a man to find a meal and a place to stay. However, he refused to give them money knowing from experience that they would only use it to buy more drink. It was his privilege to lead many of them to the Lord Jesus before they left. As a result of this, many a man went back to his wife and family; others were reunited with their parents.

From time to time Billy Sunday would receive offers with good salaries from various people. Each time, he reanalyzed his job of $83 a month at the YMCA and wondered if, in fairness to himself and his family, he should consider either another baseball contract or some other work. But each time he decided that God had led him there and he stayed. However, after three years with the YMCA in Chicago, Billy Sunday joined Rev. J. Wilbur Chapman, a well-known evangelist, arranging meetings, organizing choirs, and erecting the tents. At times he was even given an opportunity to speak from the platform, sell songbooks, assist in the offering, and help in other ways.

In December of 1895, J. Wilbur Chapman decided to give up his work as an evangelist and return to the pastorate. Now Billy Sunday was out of work not knowing which way to turn. At this time he had a wife and two children (eventually there were four: Helen, George, William, and Paul). He could not go back into baseball; he could not go back to his job at the YMCA. What could he do? He asked the Lord for guidance, and in a short time a telegram came from a small town in Iowa, asking him to come and conduct some meetings. This seemed to be the beginning of his evangelistic work.

Even though Billy Sunday did not have a publicity man on his team, the newspapers throughout the world publicized his meetings. After he had fixed a date at some city for evangelistic services, he encouraged the church people to organize. It usually started with home prayer meetings. This was done in such an organized way that they had cottage prayer meetings in every section of the city. In one city more than 84 prayer groups were held before the services began.

In most of the evangelistic campaigns, he had an usher committee, a business women's committee, a building committee, a nursery committee, a personal workers' committee, a decorating committee, and a prayer meeting committee. In some cases he actually built a special tabernacle for his meetings. It had an open roof and a sawdust floor—thus the term "sawdust trail." No board was held in place with more than two nails and a door was open at each aisle so the people could get out easily in case of fire. Billy Sunday did not believe in placing a balcony in his churches, for he felt it would make it too hard for the converts to come forward when the invitation was given.

The three most important groups of the Billy Sunday organization were the choir, the ushers, and the personal workers. The ushers were drilled and disciplined to take care of any emergency. In addition to taking the offering and ushering in the people, they also assisted the police officers to keep the overflow crowd under control. Most people would try to press into the crowded tabernacle beyond what was legally allowed in a building. The personal workers were busy at the end of the service taking care of those who came to accept Christ as their own personal Saviour.

In addition to the evening services, Billy Sunday's group conducted noon factory meetings, meetings for business women, and luncheon meetings; he attended services in the schools, the jails, and the hospitals, together with his singers and workers. Some of the people who assisted him in his work and whose names are well known today were: Homer A. Rodeheaver, B. D. Ackley, and Grace Saxe.

Billy Sunday was known to be "individualistic, unconventional, and sensational" in preaching, but very effective, with some 300,000 converts in his ministry. He was never considered a pastor or a shepherd, but rather a soldier. He was not one who comforted but one who shouted, "Arise; repent." He talked to the people in the tabernacles as he would talk on the baseball field. His words were the type heard on the street corner, the shops, the athletic field, and he was often considered undignified.

Sunday was criticized by many because of his tactics and methods. Some people thought he was too pointed. He called adultery—adultery and sin—sin, explaining, "I want the people to know what I mean." But even those who criticized his methods would have to admit that Billy Sunday "delivered the goods" and that he helped people get right with God.

Billy hit the liquor dealer and saloon keeper about as hard as anyone. He was often heard to say, "If there is anything that makes me sick, it is to have some red-nosed, buttermilk-eyed, beetle-browed, peanut-brained, stall-fed saloon keeper say that he wouldn't be in the business if it were not for the church members voting for him." The brewers of that day spent large sums of money attacking him and circulating propaganda that was slanderous. In the state of Illinois, as a result of some of his preaching, 1,500 saloons were put out of business in one day. In 11 out of 15 towns in that same state where he had campaigned, "dry" victories were won at the following election. But Billy Sunday's mission was not to preach against the saloon keeper; it was to win men and women to the Lord Jesus. However, many of his converts and friends did become temperance workers.

Billy Sunday was known as the athletic-type preacher. He was dramatic, brilliant, and humorous and paced rapidly back and forth on the platform. It was said that he traveled more than a mile over the platform every time he delivered a sermon and over 100 miles on the platform in every campaign. During his sermon he hit his hand on the pulpit, stomped his foot on the floor, and used every method of gymnastics possible in order to make a point. Not only did he use his voice, but every muscle of his body. Mr. Sunday dramatized each point he tried to make. If he was talking about a four-footed animal, he would get down on all fours; if he talked about a man who was praying, he dropped to his knees. Newspaper and advertising men of the day made cartoon sketches of Mr. Sunday's actions on the platform.

Each time, he preached as though there were someone in the audience who would never have another chance, and this is exactly how Billy Sunday felt. If perchance there was a man or woman there who would not be alive by the next sermon, he wanted to be sure to make the way of salvation clear to them so that they would know God's way and not have an excuse on the Judgment Day. He was known to have said, "If a man goes to hell, he ought to be there or he wouldn't be there."

While some evangelists were known to use tear-jerking tactics, Billy Sunday did not believe in it. He often made his people laugh, but very rarely made them cry. He showed the sinner what he was and actually made him seem absurd, foolish, wicked, and definitely ashamed of himself. In spite of the fact that Billy Sunday's voice was husky and anything but beautiful, more than 25,000 persons would come to hear him at a time.

While some people thought Billy Sunday was a man who loved the limelight, those who really knew him knew that he was not. In fact, he would not take a room in a hotel for fear that he would be pointed out or stared at. Instead, he hired a furnished house where he and his associates would stay for the entire campaign. They lived in a family-like style, bringing with them a cook to take care of the meals. Mrs. Sunday, better known as "Ma," took care of the home and was responsible for many of the details for the services.

Reporters and policemen who were assigned to the meetings were gripped by the messages of salvation presented by Billy Sunday. When the invitation was given, it was not a rare sight to see reporters and policemen going down the sawdust trail.

While Mr. Sunday used every modern method he could think of, he was very careful to stick to the old-time truths from the Bible. He made it clear that God's Word says that everyone is lost without Christ, and only by accepting Christ as Saviour can he be assured of a home in heaven. Billy Sunday did not pretend to be an educated theologian. In fact, he often said this about himself: "I don't know any more about theology than a jackrabbit does about Ping-Pong, but I'm on my way to glory." He insisted that it was not theology that saved, but Jesus Christ. He stressed that nobody was kept out of heaven because he did not understand theology.

Billy Sunday felt strongly that those who were truly converted would show changed lives as a result, such as loving their neighbors, no more gossip, paying their debts, and having family devotions. This, to Billy Sunday, proved a change that only Jesus Christ could give. He insisted that reformation was not enough, but that one had to be converted.

Whenever anyone would tell Billy Sunday that people could not be converted in one of these meetings, he insisted that people were converted in various ways. Moody accepted Christ in a shoestore; Dr. Chapman was saved in a Sunday school; Charles Finney was out in the woods praying when he was converted; Sam Jones accepted Christ at the bedside of his dying father; Gypsy Smith made his profession of faith in his father's tent; and Martin Luther crawled up a flight of stairs in Rome.

"The way to judge a tree," said Mr. Sunday, "is by its fruit."

When people would come down the aisle seeking to find God's way of salvation, Mr. Sunday would try to take the hand of each convert. Sometimes this meant shaking hands with 500 or 600 people, but he did not seem to mind. One newspaper reporter watched Mr. Sunday one night when 500 people came to the altar and reported that Billy Sunday shook hands with 57 people each minute. He did not show any partiality or prejudice. It could be a little African American boy or a well-dressed society woman. It could be a member of some baseball team or a commoner. Young or old, sick or well, prominent or unknown, he would try to take their hands. During the invitation Homer Rodeheaver, soloist for the Billy Sunday team, would often go to the piano and play and sing one of the great invitation songs.

Even though Billy Sunday had good results in his meetings, he was sometimes criticized by other ministers and Christian workers. They did not like the way he preached, the methods he used, or his choice of words. They did not like the fact that he spoke on evangelism so much, but nobody seemed to criticize his results. They had to admit that God was using him, and people were coming to know the Saviour through his efforts.

After Billy Sunday left a city, Bible study classes were set up, and the new converts attended the services in order to grow in the Lord. Also, as a result of the Billy Sunday meetings, many people purchased Bibles. In fact, one publisher complained because the Billy Sunday campaigns did not create a demand for religious books. He had to admit, "You can't sell anything but Bibles to that Billy Sunday crowd." Mr. Sunday encouraged his people to read the Bible and dig into it for spiritual truths. He often used the illustration of the diamond mines in South Africa and told the people that people all over the world knew about these diamond mines, but only those who would go there to dig for them got the diamonds.

At every Billy Sunday campaign there was music. A large choir was organized at the campaigns and was trained to bring a message in song at all the services. The congregation, too, had a chance to join in the singing of their favorite hymns.

While a few of the theologians and ministers of the various cities criticized his praying, most people enjoyed hearing Billy Sunday pray. Some said, "He talks to Jesus just as though he were talking to one of his associates." Many times while he was praying he would forget the name of someone that he wanted to remember. He would stop, turn to his songleader, and ask, "Rodie, what is the name of that person?" and then continue his praying, mentioning by name the one of whom he was thinking. Praying was not a form or a habit; it was a matter of talking with the Lord.

Billy Sunday allowed himself one month to six weeks every year for quiet and relaxation. But the rest of the time the evangelist spoke as though he were on the verge of a complete collapse. It was often said of him that he spoke "as a dying man to dying men." Going from one end of the country to the other, he gave everything he had in order to preach the Gospel of Christ.

Billy Sunday spent his last days at Winona Lake, Indiana, and on November 6, 1935, went to be with his Saviour. During his preaching career, he conducted over 300 revivals with an estimated one million who "hit the sawdust trail" to profess conversion.

God used this former major league baseball player, who was willing to set aside money and prominence, in order to bring the message of salvation to people of every status and position in life.

Robert Moffat

Robert Moffat was a pioneer missionary to Africa. He was born of poor parents in Ormiston, Scotland, in 1795. In his home he was taught the regular school subjects as well as to play the violin.

When Moffat left home, his father gave him some parting words that he never forgot: "Work hard, Bob, and keep up your studies." This became a challenge to Robert, and he tried to apply it in everything he did. His mother also left him with some unforgettable parting words: "Read a chapter of the Bible every morning and another every evening."

All these things were to benefit him later on the mission field.

Soon after his conversion he became interested in missions and applied to the London Missionary Society. Because of his lack of education, he was refused. However, after some special instruction, he was accepted and sent to Capetown, South Africa.

In 1816 after a long and dangerous voyage, Robert Moffat finally reached the land where he was to spend most of his life. Arriving in the country, he then traveled 600 miles inland by wagon and oxen. This meant crossing many rivers and swamps. The intense heat, together with the possible attacks of wild beasts, made the trip very dangerous, but he knew that God had called him to this land, and nothing could discourage him from continuing his journey. He had a party of African men with him, and from them he learned the language.

In 1817 he left for Namaqualand, the home of the notorious outlaw, Afrikaner. To the surprise of everyone, Robert Moffat won the dreaded outlaw to Christ. Afrikaner died soon after that, but the story of his conversion has ever since been a vibrant testimony of the work of grace on the mission field.

As Moffat continued his journey from tribe to tribe, he saw that elderly people were often treated very cruelly. Sometimes they were left in the desert with only enough food for one meal. It was through Moffat's teaching that the nationals learned to take care of their elderly.

After he had been on the field one year, Moffat sent to London for Mary Smith, the girl to whom he was engaged. They were married, and for the next 50 years Mary Moffat assisted in the missionary work of her husband. God blessed this marriage with a baby girl. Little did they realize that this "little lady" would eventually marry David Livingstone, the great missionary and explorer to Africa.

One day, as Robert Moffat was making a trip, he found a group of men digging a grave for a woman who had just died. The woman left two very young children. To his surprise and horror, Moffat learned that the natives were about to bury the children with their dead mother. Immediately he took the children and made them a regular part of his family.

After many years of difficult work, the ministry of Robert Moffat began to show results with more and more converts. Because of this, Mr. Moffat began to work on the construction of a written language. When the vocabulary was finally finished, he began translating the New Testament. This was a long, slow process. It was during this time that Mary Moffat became seriously ill and the Moffats returned to Capetown. While there, Moffat decided that his translation had to be printed. When he approached the government about it, officials told him he could have machinery, but no men. So, with the help of a friend, Robert Moffat began to learn the field of printing. Painstakingly he set the type himself, handling each individual letter.

Moffat was finally able to give the people of Africa both the Old and New Testaments and the story, *Pilgrim's Progress*, in their own language. In addition, while on the field, he authored a hymnbook and wrote two missionary books on South Africa.

While watching one group of people, Moffat found that the native instructors used the idea of music in teaching the alphabet. The tune they used was "Auld Lang Syne," singing it over and over again using A, B, C. (Try it; it works.)

The work of Robert Moffat continued to grow. As it grew, his fame spread. Invitations from villages all over the continent began to come, asking him to bring them the message of God. Copies of the New Testament became even more important in reaching people for Christ.

After many years in South Africa, Robert and Mary Moffat decided to return home for their first furlough. Arriving in England in 1839, they found everything except rest. The missionary's fame had even spread to England. Meeting after meeting was conducted as invitations came. Although he found this very tiring, it also gave him many opportunities to further the cause of missions in Africa.

It was while in England that Robert Moffat met David Livingstone. The younger man was also interested in missions.

"Where do you hope to go?" asked Moffat.

"China," replied Livingstone.

"Why China?" asked Moffat. Then he began to talk to Livingstone about the needs of Africa. He explained that he, an older missionary, could point the way, but the younger men would march along and accomplish the work.

A few months later Livingstone sailed for the "dark continent" and began his work of missions.

When Mr. and Mrs. Moffat returned to the field, they learned that David Livingstone had been attacked by a lion and that his left arm was badly injured. He was brought to the Moffat home and cared for by the young Mary Moffat. Months later, when David recovered, he and Mary were married and they went north to another part of Africa to do their own missionary work.

Robert and Mary Moffat had many tragic days ahead of them. First, their oldest son died; shortly after this, word came from David Livingstone that his wife, Mary, had died from fever. In spite of numerous discouragements, the Moffats continued their missionary and translation work.

Robert Moffat was now well past 70 and becoming very weary. One day he preached his last sermon in the little village church he had helped to build, and then he and his wife began their trip home to England. The year was 1870. The next year Mary Moffat went to be with the Lord. The elderly missionary was saddened by his wife's death, but continued working, writing, lecturing, and preaching until he was well over 80 years of age. In 1872 Edinburgh University honored him with the degree of Doctor of Divinity.

One night as he sat in bed, he picked up his watch and wound it. "This is the last time," he said. And it was, for the next morning, August 10, 1883, at the age of 88, Robert Moffat went to be with the Lord. His work in Africa and Britain was finished.

Charles H. Spurgeon

Charles Spurgeon's father, John, was a minister. His grandfather, James, was also a minister. So it is not surprising that Charles should follow in their footsteps. Charles Haddon Spurgeon was born on June 19, 1834, in Kelveden, Essex, England, but the early years of his life were lived with his grandparents, Rev. and Mrs. James Spurgeon. There were seventeen members of the Spurgeon family, though nine of them died in infancy. Charles' father preached on Sundays, a job that he held for sixteen years. He worked in the coal yard during the week.

When Charles was eighteen months old he went to live with his grandparents at Stambourne. For 54 years James Spurgeon ministered to the people who worshiped in the meetinghouse. Charles' "Aunt Ann" spent much time with him helping him to write and memorize. At the age of seven he returned home to his parents, but still spent most of his vacations with his grandparents.

Those early Stambourne years gave color to his life. Leaving his grandfather was the sorrow of his early days. When he returned home to Colchester, he found two more sisters and a brother, and naturally he became their hero.

At first he attended a school that was held by a Mrs. Cook, but having mastered all that she could teach him, he was transferred to a more advanced place. Here he gained the First Class English Prize when he was between ten and eleven years old.

When Charles was fourteen he and his brother were sent to St. Augustine's at Maidstone, where his uncle was one of the tutors. Charles quickly mastered his studies there too.

By the time he was fifteen years old, he had made a great deal of progress in reading, writing, arithmetic, spelling, Greek and Latin grammar, and philosophy. His mathematical ability was so outstanding at this time that he was allowed to calculate the tables that are still in use in one of the life insurance companies of London.

Young Spurgeon continued searching for five years—from the time when he was ten or eleven years old until he was between fifteen and sixteen he learned more of the things that matter than most people learn in a lifetime.

"I must confess," he said, "that I never would have been saved if I could have helped it. As long as I could, I rebelled, revolted, and struggled against God. When He would have me pray, I would not pray, and when He would have me listen to the sound of the ministry, I would not. And when I heard, and the tear rolled down my cheek, I wiped it away and defied Him to melt my soul. But long before I began with Christ, He began with me."

It was to his mother that he owed his first interest in spiritual things. Her prayers and counseling made him feel concern for his soul. Every Sunday evening Mrs. Spurgeon would gather the children around the table, and as they read the Scripture, she would explain it to them verse by verse. Then she prayed, and Charles declared that the children never forgot some of the words of her prayers.

Charles Haddon Spurgeon accepted the Lord Jesus as his Saviour on January 6, 1850. It was a snowy day. He was on his way to a certain church, but because of the storm he stopped at one a little nearer. As he entered, he found that there were less than fifteen people in the congregation. When the minister did not show up because of the storm, a shoemaker got up to "pinch-hit." He preached his sermon from Isaiah 45:22, "Look unto me, and be ye saved, all the ends of the earth." While preaching, the so-called minister pointed his finger at young Charles and said, "Young man, you're in trouble. Look to Jesus Christ. Look! Look! Look!" Charles Spurgeon did, as he gave his heart and life to the Lord. On the same Sunday, he also made the decision to enter into the ministry. On his mother's birthday, May 3, 1851, Charles followed the Lord in baptism. He said, "Conscience has convinced me that it is a duty to be buried with Christ in baptism, although I am sure it constitutes no part of salvation."

Charles began working for the Lord immediately, teaching a Sunday school class of boys, distributing tracts, and visiting the poor.

"There is no time for work like the first hours of the day and no time for serving the Lord like the earliest days of youth," said Spurgeon. He would rise early in the morning in order to read the Word of God and pray, and then he would spend the rest of the day studying. Evenings were spent teaching the Word of God. At the age of sixteen he joined an organization called, "The Lay Preachers Association," and preached his first sermon in a cottage near Cambridge. Fame of the "Boy Preacher" spread. Soon he was preaching in chapels, cottages, and open-air meetings in as many as thirteen stations in villages surrounding Cambridge. This was done in the evenings after his school duties were over.

In 1852 he accepted his first pastorate in Waterbeach, six miles from Cambridge. The church, which was originally a barn, was equipped with benches and a pulpit. On his first Sunday, there were less than a dozen people in the audience, but this soon grew. His salary at the church was $225 a year plus food that the people would bring to him from time to time. Spurgeon continued pastoring this church for two and a half years. When he began his work in the church, he found drunkenness, profanity, and much sin in the town, but this soon changed. Sunday after Sunday the little chapel was packed and people began confessing their sins and getting right with God.

A laborer's wife was Spurgeon's first convert, and he prized that soul more than all the others that came after. "I felt like a boy who had earned his first guinea, or like a diver who had been down to the depth of the sea and brought up a rare pearl."

At the age of nineteen Spurgeon gave a speech to the Cambridge Sunday School Union. He was severely criticized by the older men, who said he had no business trying to teach his seniors. They told him he should have stayed with his church at least until he was old enough to grow a beard. However, as a result of this speech, he received an invitation from a church in London. This was one of the leading Baptist churches, one of the six that had a membership of over 300. It held an honored place. The location of the chapel was very unfavorable, and as a result, the attendance had been declining for years. For three months the pastorate had been vacant. One of the men who heard him, a deacon in the London church, went back to his people and said, "If you want to fill your empty pews, send for a young man I heard in Cambridge by the name of Spurgeon."

Young Spurgeon was so surprised to receive the invitation to become the pastor of this large church that he wrote a letter telling them that it must have been a mistake. But by return mail he received word saying, "You are the one. No mistake." Still wondering, he arranged to preach at New Park Street on December 18, 1853. After a very unsympathetic reception, he was tempted to evade the appointed task at the last moment. But once in front of the congregation, which was very sparse (about eighty people), he gained confidence.

The news of the wonderful young man from the country spread. Visits were paid to friends during the afternoon, urging them to come in the evening, and a greatly increased congregation then gathered. Among them was the young woman who was later to become his wife.

The people were so excited that they would not move until the deacons assured them that they would do their best to invite the young preacher to come again. Before Spurgeon left the building, he was urged to repeat the visit.

No other preacher who supplied the pulpit at New Park Street during the vacant months had been invited a second time, but Spurgeon came again on the first, third, and fifth Sundays of January 1854. So great was the success of his ministry that on January 25, he was invited to occupy the pulpit for six months, with a view to permanent acceptance of the pastorate. Before the six months were up, the deacons of the church asked for a special church meeting. The church passed a resolution inviting Spurgeon to be their minister permanently.

Almost from the very beginning of this work at the New Park Street Chapel, the church was packed to the doors. For six consecutive Sunday evenings not only was the chapel filled but also the streets all around the church. People even had to go around to the side streets. All of this was very hard on Charles Spurgeon, for he had not as yet developed a "big crowd voice." Sometimes his voice almost gave out on him. By the end of the year, however, he had mastered the secret of projecting his voice to a large audience. Time and time again, the church was worked on to make it larger, but in a very short time it was again too small.

One Sunday evening when the hall was completely packed and 10,000 people were on the outside, the call of fire was given. A terrible panic took hold of the people and seven were killed. Twenty-eight others were seriously hurt. This experience touched Spurgeon very much. He was so upset that he spent night and day in tears over it. However, as a result, he became an outstanding preacher, and all of London now wanted to hear him. For the next three years he preached to crowds of 10,000 every Sunday. He continued to preach in the largest available buildings in England, Scotland, Ireland, and Wales. He also began outdoor services. By the time he was 22, he was the most popular preacher of his day.

When he came to the New Park Street Church in 1854, the membership was 232. At the end of 1891, 14,460 others had been baptized and added to the church. The membership then stood at 5,311.

In March 1861, the Metropolitan Tabernacle was completed, and for the next 31 years, approximately 5,000 people assembled there every Sunday morning and evening to hear Spurgeon preach. The buildings were so jammed that Spurgeon finally asked his regular attendants to stay away from the next service. They did, but the Tabernacle was still filled to capacity. On October 7, 1857, when Spurgeon was 23 years old, the largest available building was used and 23,654 people attended the service. Spurgeon was so completely exhausted as a result of the strain of this service that he slept from Wednesday to Friday morning following the meeting.

Even though the Spurgeon crowds were mostly common people, there were some of nobility too. Queen Victoria came in disguise; statesmen, soldiers, authors, artists, and ministers also came.

While pastoring the New Park Street Chapel Church, Spurgeon noticed a very attractive young lady in the audience. On January 8, 1856, this lady became Mrs.

Charles Haddon Spurgeon. God blessed their marriage and Susannah Spurgeon gave birth to twin boys, Charles and Thomas.

The home life was ideal, though Mrs. Spurgeon was bothered by frequent suffering, yet the home was never marred by fretfulness or strain. It was a deep joy to the parents when the sons were baptized, a great satisfaction when they began to preach in a cottage in Wandsworth. Both entered business careers, one in a city merchant's office, the other as an engraver on wood, but their preaching power developed.

Charles, the older, after pastorates at Greenwich, Nottingham, Cheltenham, and Hove, became his father's successor at Spurgeon's Orphanage. Thomas, the younger, after his ministry in Australia and New Zealand, became his father's successor at the Tabernacle, and carried on the work there for fourteen years. On October 20, 1917, he died.

Because Susannah Spurgeon became an invalid, she was no longer able to travel with her husband. She died on October 22, 1903.

It is said that Charles Spurgeon had more than 3,500 different sermons. His Sunday sermons were sold by tons. Aside from regular pastoral and preaching duties and publishing a weekly sermon from 1855 on, he founded the Pastors' College. Spurgeon built a circle of Sunday schools and churches, was the president of a society for distribution of Bibles and tracts, and established the Stockwell Orphanage with twelve houses that accommodated some 500 children.

Spurgeon's last sermon was preached in the Metropolitan Tabernacle on Sunday, June 7, 1891. He was only 56 years old, but he was extremely weary. The lines on his face and his white hair showed that he was an old man in spite of his years. Toward the very end of his life he said to his wife, "Oh, Wifey, I have had such a blessed time with my Lord." Then on January 31, 1892, after 40 years of ministry, Charles Haddon Spurgeon went to be with his Saviour. This took place in Mentone, France, where he had gone for his health.

On February 4, a memorial service was conducted at Mentone, and then the body was brought to the Pastors' College in Victoria Station, London, where it remained that afternoon. At night it was carried into the Tabernacle, and there the next day some sixty thousand persons passed to pay their respect to Mr. Spurgeon.

Today the Tabernacle Church still continues; the college is still training men to preach the Gospel; and the orphanage, in a new location, still houses and educates girls and boys.

So, the work of Charles Haddon Spurgeon continues.

David Brainerd

David Brainerd was the third son in a family of nine. He had four sisters and four brothers. Their home was in Haddam, Connecticut.

David was a very shy boy and found it difficult to express himself. He could not even find enough courage to confide in his parents, so he kept to himself the questions that puzzled and often worried him. He realized at a very early age that things were not right between him and God, and the thought of death terrified him.

David was nine years old when his father passed away, and when David was fourteen his mother died. These deaths brought many more questions and puzzles to the mind of David Brainerd. The question that bothered him most of all was how he could know God. He knew *about* God, but he was not sure he really knew God and continually felt that there was something missing in his life.

David attended church regularly and spent a great deal of time reading the Bible and in prayer, but God seemed to be as far away as ever, and there was no peace and joy in his heart. He knew he was still not right with God and wondered what else he could do.

At the age of nineteen, he went to work on a farm in Durham. He stayed there about a year and during that year, decided to live a rigid, religious life. Of this time he wrote, "I became very strict over my thoughts, words, and actions, and I imagined that I did dedicate myself to the Lord." Still he found that he was not a happy person.

Shortly after his twenty-first birthday, the truth of salvation was made clear to him. He did not have to work for his salvation. Christ had paid the penalty of sin when He died on the cross of Calvary. All God wanted David to do was accept this salvation personally and commit his life to God. This he did on July 12, 1739, and from that moment on his entire life was changed. Now all he wanted to do was spend his life in service for Christ.

In September 1739, Brainerd entered Yale College at New Haven in order to begin his training. But in his third year at college, he was expelled. This caused much excitement among the students because David was a brilliant student and one of the most outstanding Christians on campus. It all came about one day when David and a few close friends were talking together. They were freely discussing one of their teachers who had disapproved of the prayer meetings the Christian students held among themselves. One of the boys asked David what he thought of the teacher. He replied hotly, "He has no more grace than this chair!" Unknown to the group, another student had overhead them and word soon got back to the school authorities. They told David he would either have to make a public confession and humble himself before the college or leave. He refused to apologize and was expelled immediately. Four years later, he wrote a public confession and apologized before the entire college.

After his dismissal, he went to live with a pastor with whom he continued his studies. While there, he gave a great deal of thought to what he would do with his life. He still wanted to spend it in the service of God. If he couldn't be a minister, maybe he could be a missionary. As time went on, he became more convinced that missionary work was God's will for his life. Soon he was appointed by a Scottish missionary society to begin a work among the Native Americans of New York, New Jersey, and Pennsylvania.

The first thing he had to do was learn a very difficult language. This required a great deal of patience, and the study was very slow, especially since the language was divided into many different dialects. He never became very fluent in the language, so he had to rely mostly on Native Americans, who could speak some English, to interpret for him.

Not only were his lessons slow, but his acceptance by the people was exceptionally slow because they were suspicious of him. In the past they had often been mistreated by the white man and, therefore, trusted none of them.

Another difficulty that David Brainerd had in working with the Native Americans was the influence of their pow-wows. Magicians, who claimed to have all kinds of mysterious powers, recognized that the more David preached to the people, the more light of the Gospel began to spread among them. This, of course, meant that they questioned the work of the magicians and would rather put their faith and trust in Christ. As a result, these evil men made it very difficult not only for the native Believers, but for Brainerd as well.

The success of Brainerd's ministry is undoubtedly due to his outstanding prayer life. It seemed almost as natural for David to pray as to breathe, and he often spent all night in prayer. He had many days of disappointment and often became dejected or depressed over the situations in his work with the Native Americans. They did not seem to respond to God's message of love in the way he had hoped they would.

Few have sacrificed so much and so cheerfully as David Brainerd in order to take the Gospel to the heathen. For almost the whole of his missionary life, he was cut off from the companionship of friends. He had no comforts, was frequently exposed to danger, and often had difficulty in obtaining suitable food. Despite all these trials, not once did he think of giving up.

He was sickly much of the time, and during his illnesses he had no one to care for him. This brought about much discouragement and despondency.

One of David's interpreters learned much about the Lord Jesus in this work. Brainerd was quite sure that the young man had not accepted Christ as Saviour, but he noticed that the message greatly impressed him. One day he came to David in great distress and asked, "What must I do to be saved?" Brainerd gave this young man the same answer Paul had once given to the jailer of Philippi, "Believe on the Lord Jesus Christ, and thou shalt be saved." This young man became David's most faithful and valuable worker. He was not only his translator, but was also able to help David understand the ideas and customs of the Native American people.

God blessed the ministry of this missionary to the Native Americans in a miraculous way. Suddenly, and David knew not why, many Native Americans began coming to the meetings and asking for spiritual help. This revival began in the summer of 1745. For several weeks they continued to come in large numbers, and many of them responded to the invitation. For the first time, David saw a breakthrough in his ministry. The highlight of this revival came on August 8.

On that day people of every age and size were in attendance. Many of them had been notorious drunkards for years, but now they came to hear the message of salvation and give themselves to the Saviour. David had a sincere love for the Native Americans, and they realized that he had given up everything in order to bring the message of salvation to them.

On October 9, 1747, David Brainerd died of tuberculosis. Though not yet thirty years of age, his work was done, and he went home to be with the Lord.